IRELAND IN THE WAR YEARS AND AFTER

1939 – 51

IRELAND IN THE
WAR YEARS
AND AFTER
1939-51

Edited by

Kevin B. Nowlan
and
T. Desmond Williams

GILL AND MACMILLAN

First published 1969

Gill and Macmillan Limited
2 Belvedere Place
Dublin 1

SBN 7171 0271 8

Cover design by Desmond Fitzgerald

Printed and bound in the Republic of Ireland by Cahill & Co. Limited.

Contents

CONTRIBUTORS   vii

PREFACE   ix

ON THE EVE OF THE WAR   *Kevin B. Nowlan*   1

IRELAND AND THE WAR   *T. Desmond Williams*   14

THE IRISH ECONOMY DURING THE WAR
   James Meenan   28

IRISH DEFENCE POLICY, 1938-51
   G. A. Hayes-McCoy   39

ULSTER DURING THE WAR AND AFTER
   David Kennedy   52

THE YEARS OF READJUSTMENT, 1945-51
   F. S. L. Lyons   67

EDUCATION AND LANGUAGE, 1938-51
   Donal McCartney   80

INDUSTRY AND LABOUR   *Donal Nevin*   94

CHURCH AND STATE IN MODERN IRELAND
                    R. Dudley Edwards   109

THE CHANGING PATTERN OF IRISH SOCIETY,
1938–51   *Gerard Quinn*   120

IRISH FOREIGN POLICY, 1945-51
                    Nicholas Mansergh   134

THE IRISH PARTY SYSTEM, 1938-51
                    John A. Murphy   147

LITERATURE AND SOCIETY, 1938-51
                    Augustine Martin   167

THE IRISH ECONOMY SINCE THE WAR, 1946-51
                    Patrick Lynch   185

CONCLUSION   *T. Desmond Williams*   201

INDEX   213

Contributors

R. DUDLEY EDWARDS   Professor of Modern Irish History, University College, Dublin.

G. A. HAYES-McCOY   Professor of History, University College, Galway.

DAVID KENNEDY   Formerly of St Malachy's College, Belfast.

PATRICK LYNCH   Associate Professor of Political Economy, University College, Dublin.

F. S. L. LYONS   Professor of Modern History, University of Kent at Canterbury.

DONAL McCARTNEY   Lecturer in Modern Irish History, University College, Dublin.

NICHOLAS MANSERGH   Smuts Professor of Commonwealth History, University of Cambridge.

AUGUSTINE MARTIN   Lecturer in English, University College, Dublin.

JAMES F. MEENAN   Professor of Political Economy and National Economics, University College, Dublin.

JOHN A. MURPHY	Lecturer in Irish History, University College, Cork.
DONAL NEVIN	Assistant General Secretary, Irish Congress of Trade Unions.
KEVIN B. NOWLAN	Associate Professor of Modern History, University College, Dublin.
GERARD QUINN	Lecturer in Political Economy, University College, Dublin.
T. DESMOND WILLIAMS	Professor of Modern History, University College, Dublin.

Preface

The fifteen contributions to this volume were originally broadcast in the Thomas Davis Lecture series from Radio Éireann between January and April 1967. Since then, the authors of the lectures have had an opportunity of revising the texts. In some instances the lectures have been fully rewritten, in others additional material has been incorporated in the texts.

Until much more source material is made available, especially from state archives, in Ireland and elsewhere, it will be difficult to write definitive accounts of certain aspects of our recent history, particularly in relation to political and diplomatic developments. A beginning, however, must be made. We trust that these present studies may help towards a better understanding of a period in which Ireland was subject to the pressures and uncertainties of a world at war and to the harsh challenges of the confused post-war years.

Many important problems such as partition, emigration, rural depopulation and industrial underdevelopment still remained unresolved by the end of our period, but the years between 1939 and 1951 had, at least, demonstrated the viability of an Irish state in a time of great stress and danger.

On the Eve of the War

Kevin B. Nowlan

The opening months of the year 1938, in Ireland at least, were a time of relative peace and perhaps optimism. The new Constitution had come into operation on 29 December 1937 and the sometimes heated, sometimes unreal debates about its merits and demerits were over. It was symptomatic of the acceptance of the new order that, when the first President of Ireland had to be elected, the political parties were quickly able to find an agreed candidate in the Protestant scholar, Dr Douglas Hyde, who was formally returned without opposition on 4 May. The creation of the office of President was clearly not a step towards dictatorship as some of the critics of the draft constitution had feared. As important, in practical terms, as this constitutional settlement, in helping to give an air of greater stability to Irish life, in 1938, was the successful outcome of the Anglo-Irish negotiations.

The talks had begun, on the initiative of the Irish government, early in January. They were protracted and, with interruptions, they lasted until 25 April, when the Anglo-Irish agreements were signed in London. These discussions were particularly important because a great deal, as it proved, was at stake; not merely the ending of the costly and protracted economic war, but also such issues as partition and the occupation of certain ports in Ireland by British forces. We know that the Irish delegation, led by Mr de Valera, went to London determined to cover the whole range of the outstanding differences between the two countries. Priority, in the discussions, was apparently given to partition and related problems and to the question of the continuance of the military facilities which the British could claim under the terms of the 1921 treaty. On the economic side, the land annuities dispute and the punitive customs duties imposed during the economic war were among the most urgent issues discussed.

The negotiations were at times difficult and on the partition question certainly unproductive, for no progress was made towards the unification of Ireland politically. Indeed, the prospects, in February, seemed most gloomy. Returning from London, on 26 February Mr de Valera said : 'A comprehensive settlement, the only one that would have world significance, seems now almost unattainable.'[1] But the important thing was that the discussions did go on despite the disappointments.

The status of Northern Ireland remained unaltered in the final settlement and Mr de Valera did not conceal his regret at this, since he argued that the continuance of partition made it impossible to put Anglo-Irish relations on a completely normal footing. This was to be a factor of primary importance in the shaping of Irish policies during the critical closing months of 1938 and throughout 1939. But in all other respects the three agreements signed on 25 April were a substantial achievement for the Irish negotiators. The first agreement abrogated the provisions of Articles 6 and 7 of the Anglo-Irish Treaty of 1921. The practical effect of the abrogation of these articles was that the British gave up the harbour and other military and naval rights which they could exercise under the treaty, and they did so without any reservations. The second agreement provided for the payment by Ireland of £10 million to the British Exchequer as a final financial

1. On 27 February he added that, because of the partition issue, 'there can be no real reconciliation between Ireland and Britain, no matter what other agreements can be reached' (*The Irish Times*, 28 Feb. 1938).

settlement between the two countries. For their part, the British waived their claim to the land annuities and agreed to remove the special duties. The £10 million settlement was made to meet British financial claims other than the much disputed land annuities, but Mr de Valera told the Dáil,[2] 'if sheer equity was to decide these matters—instead of paying money to Britain . . . the payments should be made the other way'.[3] A compromise had to be found and it was found at a remarkably modest price.

The decision to remove the punitive tariffs opened the way for the third and, in economic terms, the most important agreement of all: The Anglo-Irish Trade Agreement. The general effect of this instrument was to open the British market again to the Irish cattle trade and to Irish food products with the minimum of restrictions. It also enabled Irish manufacturers, capable of selling in a competitive market, to sell their goods in the United Kingdom again with few restrictions. In return, possibly the most significant concession made on the Irish side was the undertaking to review all existing protective duties. The purpose of the survey, by the Prices Commission, was to put British manufacturers in a position to sell competitively on the Irish market, 'provided that in the application of this principle special consideration may be given to the case of (Irish) industries not fully established'.[4] The economic war was over. But how, in practice, would the new accord affect the industries that had gone into production, in Ireland, since 1932?

The Anglo-Irish Trade Agreement was a clear, unambiguous recognition of the close, enduring links between the British and the Irish economies, or as Mr Seán MacEntee, the then Minister for Finance, expressed it early in 1939: 'Anything, therefore, which would tend to impede the fair course of trade between the two countries, anything which would create enmity between the two peoples . . . is a matter of

2. The *Dáil* is the lower house of the Irish parliament.
3. *Dáil Éireann, Parliamentary Debates,* lxxi, 41–2.
4. *Irish Press,* 26 April 1938.

the gravest concern to every one of us, but most of all to those, who are the mainstay of Ireland, the farmers.'[5]

Not surprisingly, the Fine Gael opposition was quick to suggest that Fianna Fáil was, in effect, stealing the policies Fine Gael had long advocated, by freeing trade with Britain and by approaching tariffs and industrial protection in a more cautious fashion. The answer from Mr Seán Lemass was that the Anglo-Irish Agreement still left them free to develop their own industrial resources. And the Fianna Fáil spokesmen stressed, too, that protection was never intended to be an end in itself, but simply a means of creating viable industries and a more diversified economy; industrialization would go on. There are probably merits in both claims. In retrospect, possibly the most significant aspect of the Anglo-Irish Trade Agreement was that it did help to narrow the gap between the Fianna Fáil and the Fine Gael approaches to economic policies. The latter party might still criticize self-sufficiency and praise the conservative, deflationary recommendations of the Banking Commission, while the former might continue to stress the value of industrialization and capital expenditure on social projects, but after the Anglo-Irish Agreement things could never be quite the same as in the years of the punitive tariffs and the economic war. The Second World War came too soon to enable us to assess the full implications of the agreement. But the freer growth of trade in the post-war years, and the positive emphasis given by all parties to the value of industrial exports may well be seen as the delayed consequences of what was devised in 1938.

We now know that the British decision to give up the ports removed one of the most serious obstacles to effective Irish neutrality in time of war. In effect, the Irish state became freer than ever before to pursue an independent foreign policy. But it won this freedom of action at a dangerous time. The League of Nations was dying and with it the concept of collective security. The place of the small inde-

5. Institute of Bankers' meeting, 22 Jan., *Irish Independent*, 23 Jan. 1939.

pendent, neutral state had again become an extremely uncertain one. The evacuation of the Irish ports by the British, therefore, gave two related problems, neutrality and defence, an urgency and an importance they had not previously known in Irish politics.

In pressing for the transfer of the ports, during the London negotiations, Mr de Valera appears to have been influenced by the fact that, in the event of war, the Irish government would be placed in an intolerable position should Britain demand her full rights under Articles 6 and 7 of the 1921 treaty.[6] His government obviously could not recognize such a claim, in the given conditions. He further elaborated his opinions on this subject when he told the Dáil, on 16 February 1939, 'I do not mind reminding the House of it, that it is very difficult to remain neutral. I said that we would not be regarded as neutral by a foreign power if the Treaty conditions remained—that is if it suited the purposes of that foreign power'.[7] The British government may possibly have concluded that the Irish ports were of little military value under modern conditions. But whatever their motives in agreeing to a return of the ports, the decision certainly gave Mr de Valera and his colleagues a new freedom of action which they exercised with much judgement and diplomatic skill during the war years.

6. The Articles of Agreement for a Treaty between Great Britain and Ireland, of 6 December 1921, provided: '6. Until an arrangement has been made between the British and Irish Governments whereby the Irish Free State undertakes her own coastal defence, the defence by sea of Great Britain and Ireland shall be undertaken by His Majesty's Imperial Forces. . . . The foregoing provisions of this Article shall be reviewed at a Conference of Representatives of the British and Irish Governments to be held at the expiration of five years from the date hereof with a view to the undertaking by Ireland of a share in her own coastal defence. 7. The Government of the Irish Free State shall afford to His Majesty's Imperial Forces: (*a*) In time of peace such harbour and other facilities as are indicated in the Annex hereto, or such other facilities as may from time to time be agreed between the British Government and the Government of the Irish Free State; and (*b*) In time of war or of strained relations with a Foreign Power such harbour and other facilities as the British Government may require for the purposes of such defence as aforesaid'.

7. *Dáil Éireann, Parliamentary Debates*, lxxiv, 719.

It is necessary to examine more closely the government's attitude in 1938-9, since it was to be of the highest importance in determining Ireland's position when war began, in September 1939. As on other occasions, Mr de Valera insisted, throughout our period, that Ireland would never freely permit her territory to be used as a base for an attack by a hostile power on Great Britain. Short, therefore, of an attack by Britain on this country, there was no reason why Ireland and Britain should ever be engaged in an armed conflict. Partition was not to be solved by force. But there was a positive and a negative side to all this. The Taoiseach[8] told the Dáil on 27 April 1938: 'I have always said that in my view an independent Ireland would have interests, very many interests, in common with Great Britain. In providing for our defence of our own interests, we would also of necessity be providing to a certain extent for British defence of British interests'.[9] The obstacle, however, to any really close co-operation was, he stressed, partition. 'Let me say clearly', he told the *Evening Standard* in October 1938, 'that the chances of such co-operation in the event of a European war are very slight while partition remains. If such a war occurred while British forces were in occupation of any part of Ireland, Irish sentiment would definitely be hostile to any co-operation.'[10]

The Irish position was also complicated by the great volume of trade with Britain, a trade which was essential to the country's economic survival. In a comment as early as 29 April 1938, Mr de Valera stressed the point that 'in modern war there is not any neutrality. During the war, trade from one neutral country was stopped or interfered with by the belligerents on both sides.'[11] For a time, indeed, it appeared as though the Irish government might agree to military staff consultations with the British on a more

8. The *Taoiseach* is the Irish Prime Minister.
9. *Dáil Éireann, Parliamentary Debates*, lxxi, 38.
10. Reprinted in *Irish Independent*, 18 Oct. 1938.
11. *Dáil Éireann, Parliamentary Debates*, lxxi, 428.

or less formal basis. And Mr de Valera developed his views on neutrality and its problems still further, on 16 February 1939, when he said in the Dáil, 'It is possible that, despite any declarations on our part of our desire to keep out of these conflicts, if we desired and tried to carry on the trade which is essential to our economic life here, we would be regarded as a combatant, and our neutrality would not be respected'.[12] Given what subsequently happened in the case of countries such as Norway, Denmark and the Netherlands, this was a realistic assessment of the risks a small country was exposed to, once neutrality had ceased to have any absolute meaning. But shorn of the warnings and reservations, the government's decision was in favour of the maintenance of a rather strict neutrality as long as the powers would respect that neutrality. 'Now with due deliberation', Mr de Valera told the Dáil in May 1939, 'the Government has set the aim of its policy, in the present circumstances, to preserve a position of neutrality. We believe that no other position would be accepted by the majority of our people as long as the present position exists.'[13]

The chief opposition party, Fine Gael, did not in 1938-9 present a unified policy on the complex question of neutrality and Ireland's relations with Great Britain and the other Commonwealth countries, in the event of a major war. Fine Gael spokesmen vigorously criticized the government for failing to formulate its own neutrality policy in clear and unambiguous terms, but, at the same time, it is possible to find a wide variety of views on neutrality within the Fine Gael ranks—differences which, perhaps, reflect the composite origins of the party and the conflicting views on the moral obligations arising from Ireland's association with the British Commonwealth.

Mr John A. Costello, in July 1938, argued that while we could remain neutral in theory, it would be extremely difficult for us to keep out of the war if we were to maintain our

---

12. *Dáil Éireann, Parliamentary Debates*, lxxiv, 719.
13. *Dáil Éireann, Parliamentary Debates*, lxxv, 1462.

trade with Britain—an opinion which has some interesting affinities with views expressed on the government side. Mr James Dillon, in February 1939, urged, and in this he anticipated his later stand, that any port facilities Britain and the United States required in time of war should be given to them. In contrast, General Seán MacEoin, in March 1939, took some of his party colleagues and Mr de Valera to task. He was satisfied, he said, that neutrality was both possible and desirable. If necessary, it would be better to forgo our exports than to abandon neutrality. This was a view which the leader of the Labour Party, Mr W. Norton, came close to sharing when he said that as far as possible neutrality and isolation offered the best course in the event of war.

The interesting suggestion has been made that the failure of Fine Gael to adopt what might be described as a clear Commonwealth line at this time was of 'momentous' significance for the party, in that it became increasingly difficult to distinguish in terms of policy between Fine Gael and Fianna Fáil. Much can be said in favour of this argument, but it must also be remembered that the circumstances of the time made it increasingly difficult for any political party to adopt any policy other than one of watchful neutrality. Dislike of partition and reserve about British claims and intentions were attributes by no means confined to the leaders and supporters of any one Irish party.

Early in May 1938, the last of the political prisoners sentenced by the old military tribunal for political offences, were amnestied by the government. This was a gesture intended to emphasize the point that, under a popularly adopted constitution, there should be no need and no justification for men to have recourse to arms in the pursuit of political ends. The hopes of the administration were to be frustrated, however, by the fact that there were groups who held firmly to the belief that the Irish Republic proclaimed in 1916 and reaffirmed by Dáil Éireann in 1919 still existed and was the legitimate authority for all Ireland. As a consequence, they rejected not merely the 1922 Free State Constitution but the 1937 Constitution as well. They remained unconvinced by the argument that the British Crown was retained as an instrument in external relations in order to preserve a bridgehead with the North in the interest of winning national unity. The Dublin administration was for the republicans essentially a continuance of British rule in Ireland.

The militant republican movement had become badly divided by the mid-nineteen-thirties on questions of policy and leadership. In the course of 1938, however, determined efforts appear to have been made to give radical republicanism a more aggressive and disciplined character. There were few signs of I.R.A. activity in the first half of the year, but from the autumn onwards the situation changed rapidly. Several British customs huts on the Border were destroyed, there were reports of training activities and then a notable proclamation was published in the *Wolfe Tone Weekly* early in December. The document, signed by seven signatories claiming to be the 'Executive Council of Dáil Éireann', transferred all authority to the Army Council of the I.R.A. This move was part of a plan to strengthen the control of the militants and to lessen the possibility of differences between the civilian and the military branches of the radical republican movement. The full implications of these changes were seen when an ultimatum, dated 12 January 1939, was delivered to Lord Halifax, the British Foreign Secretary, demanding an undertaking that all British forces be withdrawn from Irish soil; otherwise the I.R.A. would 'take appropriate action'.[14]

After the expiration of the four-day ultimatum came the news of explosions and fires in Manchester, Birmingham, London and many other English centres. The bombing incendiary raids had begun and they were to reach their tragic and fatal climax in the late summer of 1939. They achieved nothing except to excite a measure of anti-Irish feeling in Britain and, indeed, it would appear the Army Council itself

14. *Wolfe Tone Weekly*, 21 Jan. 1939.

was divided on the wisdom of launching these attacks in Britain. But the I.R.A. under its Chief of Staff, Seán Russell, had once again become a potentially dangerous political factor.

The revival of extremist activity, though the numbers directly involved were small, probably owed something to the success of para-military action on the continent in undoing the post-1918 settlements. Yet a striking aspect of the I.R.A. campaign was not the fact that they had some contacts with Germany but that these contacts were so weak and rather ineffective. The Germans, for their own reasons, were slow to cultivate the I.R.A. and the conspiracy remained very much a domestic affair with some traditional Irish-American support. The lack of any serious foreign involvement may, perhaps, have made the problem easier to master, but the determined, aggressive quality of the I.R.A. campaign in England was a warning sign that 1939 was going to be, in certain ways, a more testing year than that of the Anglo-Irish agreements.

The Irish government was able to approach these challenges from a position of considerable strength in terms of parliamentary support. The general election of 1937 had deprived Fianna Fáil of its overall majority in the Dáil, and the Labour Party was the gainer from this set-back to the government's fortunes. The 1937 results, of course, reflected the depressing effects of the disputes with Britain and the worldwide economic strains. Politically Mr de Valera's ministry was left in a difficult position, depending on the Labour vote for its survival. In the summer of 1938 this situation was decisively changed.

In May 1938, a Fine Gael sponsored motion, relating to civil service arbitration procedures, was carried by a single vote in the Dáil, the Labour and Independent deputies supporting Fine Gael. Mr de Valera's reaction to this defeat was to seek and get an immediate dissolution of the Dáil, arguing that 'a government with a precarious parliamentary majority constantly at the mercy of group combinations in support of sectional interests cannot do the nation's work as it should be done'.[15]

Fianna Fáil fought the June election from a position of considerable strength. The economic war had been successfully concluded, and though unemployment remained a serious and unresolved problem throughout 1938-9, there had been a modest recovery in the volume of Irish trade since 1937. There was every reason to expect even better in the future with the reopening of the British markets on a very liberal basis. The election was fought at short notice and Fine Gael were able to derive little advantage from their claim that Fianna Fáil had now borrowed policies they had long advocated. The results, however, show that, in proportion to their numbers, it was the Labour Party rather than Fine Gael which suffered most. Once more, some of the marginal voters had transferred their allegiance from Labour to Fianna Fáil. With a majority of sixteen seats, the government had won a considerable victory.

Backed by this clear majority, the government, early in 1939, decided to counter any threat from the republican militants by putting the Offences Against the State Act through the Oireachtas.[16] This measure enabled the government to revive the military tribunal for the trial of political offences and the act also gave the state the right to intern persons without trial. The hand of authority was still further strengthened by the enactment of a new treason measure.

From March 1939 onwards, the growing danger of war in Europe and the problem of the I.R.A. inevitably determined the course of Irish political developments to a great extent. Europe was preparing for war and Britain's decision to introduce compulsory military service brought with it a sudden and dangerous crisis in Anglo-Irish relations.

Towards the end of April, it became clear that, under the terms of the British Military Training Bill, conscription

15. *Irish Press*, 28 May 1938.
16. The *Oireachtas* is the Irish Parliament.

could be extended to Northern Ireland. This threat provoked
an immediate sharp reaction in Ireland. Mr de Valera,
because of 'grave events', cancelled an official visit to the
United States; and the Catholic bishops in the North,
following the precedent set by the Irish hierarchy in 1918,
issued a strongly-worded joint pastoral. They warned that
any measures taken to compel the Catholic people to fight
for 'their oppressor would be likely to rouse their indignation
and resistance'.[17] And the danger of serious unrest was in
no way lessened by Northern Ireland's Premier, Lord
Craigavon, declaring that the loyal people of Northern
Ireland would welcome conscription. Had the British government pressed the issue, it is difficult to see how any Irish
government could have avoided an open conflict with
Britain. As it was, the government, with the support of the
other parties, protested in the strongest terms. Fortunately,
good sense soon prevailed. On 4 May, Mr Chamberlain told
the House of Commons that Northern Ireland would be
excluded from the Bill. This crisis was over. The weight and
unanimity of Irish public opinion and the close personal
understanding which had been established between the
British and Irish leaders were factors which helped to bring
the crisis to an end.

In Ireland, the years immediately preceding the outbreak
of the Second World War were not marked by a break-down
in democratic government as in so many European countries.
And though the I.R.A. remained a disturbing factor, it was
a marginal one. The tendency, in Ireland, was for conservative rather than for revolutionary forces to grow stronger.
Though the Banking Commission's majority report was not
given an enthusiastic reception in Fianna Fáil circles, it is
perhaps significant that financial practices, especially in
terms of the link with sterling, remained conventional and
respectably sound. Again, as we have seen, there was a
certain narrowing of the gap between the two major political

17. *Irish Independent,* 1 May 1939.

parties and this process was, no doubt, aided by the general acceptance of the new Constitution and by the long-term implications of the Anglo-Irish Trade Agreement. Indeed, the clarification of Ireland's constitutional position, in 1937, made easier the task of negotiating a sensible Anglo-Irish settlement in 1938.

The Anglo-Irish settlement not merely gave formal recognition to the reality of the interdependence of the British and Irish economies but also acknowledged effectively the independence of Ireland in the field of foreign policy.

Ireland and the War

T. DESMOND WILLIAMS

On 1 September 1939, German armies crossed the Polish frontier; on 2 September the Taoiseach introduced a bill to amend Article 28 of the Irish Constitution with a view to passing emergency legislation during a war in which Ireland was not involved. And on 3 September Britain and France separately declared war on Germany. World War II had begun.

On 30 April 1945, Adolf Hitler took his life in Berlin and, on 1 May, Eamon de Valera called on the German minister, Herr Eduard Hempel, and expressed his personal sympathy. The war was virtually over.

Most states in the world had become actively engaged in it. Ireland remained neutral throughout, along with Switzerland, Spain, Portugal and Sweden and a few others. At one stage or another during the years of conflict the great belligerent powers applied pressure on neutral states to abandon their neutrality, very often successfully, according to the ebb and flow of military events. Each neutral state had its own special problems, and each of them too was particularly affected by the policies of neighbouring great powers. The story of Ireland's neutrality principally concerns relations with Britain, Germany, the United States, and, to a far lesser extent, with Italy and Japan. With one other great power, Soviet Russia, she had no diplomatic relations at all. The story too is concerned not only with foreign, but also with domestic history.

14

At the outset of the war Irish neutrality, though foreshadowed by de Valera (in February 1939) and officially adopted by the Dáil (on 2 September) was by no means clearly established—in the sense, for example, that Swiss neutrality was universally recognized. Very few international observers believed it could or would ever be implemented.

Many states, for example, Norway, Denmark and Turkey, to mention only three, started out neutral, but were compelled to abandon their stand later on. In Ireland the official policy adopted by the Dáil was by no means unconditionally accepted. Particularly after the fall of France many leaders of the opposition, especially deputies Dillon, McGilligan and O'Higgins, did not seem to believe that a neutral stand could possibly be maintained. Others did not morally approve anyhow. And even in de Valera's cabinet, which was far more tightly controlled than the opposition front bench, varying views were held. There were no outright pro-Germans on that side, but there was a good deal of suspicion and hostility regarding Britain and British intentions. The changing circumstances of the war eventually modified public opinion. At the outset, and up till June 1940, the Germans, led by Hitler (who had been sharply condemned by Pius XI in 1937) were attacking Poland—a Catholic power which had, in its position with relation to its great power neighbour, Germany, certain similarities, historically speaking, to Ireland's position with relation to the United Kingdom. Many public speakers demanded that Ireland should associate herself with public disapproval of German policies designed to eliminate Catholic Poland. It was only after Italy entered the war on Germany's side in June 1940 that the balance was somewhat redressed. From then on the religious issue counted rather less—at least it served to confuse rather than clarify the development of Irish public opinion. Hitler, after all, was now not only linked with Catholic Italy; his cause was partly identified with that of Spain under Franco, of Vichy France under Pétain, and of the small state of Slovakia under Monsignor Tiso, a Catholic prelate (subsequently hanged at the end of the war).

There were five major stages of the war in so far as it involved Ireland. The first ended in June 1940, the second ran from June to November 1940, the third from November 1940 to June 1941, with the outbreak of Russo-German hostilities. Later in that year, on 11 December, another turning point was reached, when America declared war on Germany and Japan. There then followed another stage during which Germany clearly seemed to be losing. On 25 July 1943 Mussolini fell. The Russians drove the German armies slowly but remorselessly back towards their frontiers, and the allied invasion of German-occupied Europe took place on 6 June 1944. All these ups and downs had their effect on Irish policy towards the great powers, and on the policies of the powers towards Ireland herself. What were the principal developments?

In the first nine months Ireland had no great external problems of a political or economic nature. The French army was still in existence, and, in allied eyes, the French army was the strongest in the world. The Germans were far away from Irish shores and their submarine and surface fleet operations were of no real danger, as yet, to Britain and, therefore, to Ireland. As far as external relations were concerned, de Valera's principal problem was to maintain the *status quo,* guarding his stated policy of neutrality. None of the great powers at that stage were apparently concerned to have it otherwise, or, if they were, they were in no position to do anything about it. The government's chief political problems related to internal security and to keeping control of the I.R.A. Certainly neither Chamberlain nor Roosevelt nor Hitler was thinking much about Ireland then.

The entire situation radically changed with the overthrow of France. The coastal areas of Norway, Denmark, Holland, Belgium and France were now not only at the disposal certainly of the German navy and air force, but also of the German army. At this stage the geographical position of Ireland became significant to military leaders on both sides. It looked as if England might be shortly invaded and the Germans seek to land troops in Ireland as part of a general invasion of

Britain. It was no less possible that the British, in their desperation, might attempt to anticipate the Germans by seizing the southern part of Ireland, on account of its being insufficiently protected against an occupying Wehrmacht or Luftwaffe.

Again the Blitzkrieg had worked in Scandinavia. Might it not work on Irish soil as well? At this point, for the first time, de Valera and the opposition parties set about attempting to introduce some kind of effective defence force. In the same period authorized but secret conversations took place between British officers in Northern Ireland and Irish officers in the South. The civil servants started to burn some of their papers and thought of transferring Irish gold from Dublin to Foynes; and de Valera also began to seek weapons for the Irish army from Britain and America.

The arrival in Ireland in early May of an important German intelligence officer and the discovery in an I.R.A. household of military plans for the occupation of Northern Ireland added to what, in the light of subsequent knowledge, must be described as a panic. In fact those plans had not been drawn up by the Germans, and Captain Goertz, the German agent, had not been sent to direct operations against the Irish government. Still Goertz did manage to escape detection, and he was not arrested for another eighteen months. According to his own claims, he met several hundred people, including four Dáil deputies. His story is an interesting but eventually insignificant one. The German intelligence service heard from him now and again, but he had lost his transmitter on arrival, and it was only with the help of a former member of the Electricity Supply Board that he was able to re-establish communications. He tried three times to return to Germany, but failed. Sometimes Goertz thought he was in virtual control of all I.R.A. activities and reported that he could mobilize eight thousand men against the British or the Americans. This agent felt he had been let down by the Abwehr and by Canaris. He managed to keep in touch with the German Legation through the counsellor, Herr Thomsen. But the minister,

Hempel, was extremely nervous about his activities. The latter's principal objective was to avoid giving any pretext for Britain to invade the South, and here he was in accord with de Valera. He was especially anxious when he heard that Goertz had established contact with two leading Irish army officers and was also making arrangements to meet Cardinal MacRory in the late autumn of 1941. Around this time too the head of the German Secret Service, Canaris, and his principal expert on Ireland—Veesemayer—envisaged the dispatch of a German military mission to Ireland to establish contact with the I.R.A. and Goertz, if the latter was still in the country. At one stage there was talk of landing a hundred and twenty specialists to advise the I.R.A. : this number was rapidly reduced to ten and finally to three, including a former exchange student, who had spent some years in Ireland before the war. The Germans had previously tried to send Seán Russell and Frank Ryan to Ireland in the summer of 1940, but these two had not been charged with any particular military mission and neither knew anything about the other's intended role. The new scheme was potentially far more dangerous. If the British had known of it, and if it had been executed, Churchill and Roosevelt might well have had an excuse for putting much stronger pressure on the Irish government than they had in fact done up till then.

In the first two periods of the war—up to November 1940 —Hitler and Ribbentrop had taken little interest in Ireland; they had also decreed that nothing should be done to embarrass de Valera or his government. The most dramatic episode endangering neutrality—and of this de Valera was aware— involved a proposal to send two German military attachés to work in the German Legation around Christmas 1940. De Valera would have nothing to do with this plan. In fact Sir John Maffey, the British High Commissioner, came to learn of it and, if it had been accepted, British and American allegations of the German Legation in Dublin being used as a centre for espionage would have had sounder foundation. Hempel too was strongly against the idea and agreed with de Valera that it could well prove to be the thin end of the wedge regarding Anglo-American intervention. De Valera gained his point and that particular crisis was over by the spring of 1941. There remained, however, one other serious point: namely the presence in the German Legation at Northumberland Road of a radio transmitter.

The transmitter had been used from time to time by the Germans for the purpose of weather reports. The British and the Irish intelligence services were well aware of its existence; the British naturally asserted that it was being, or certainly could be, used for ordinary espionage purposes. International law was obscure on the legality of this particular practice. Certainly the British used their own transmitters in neutral countries such as Switzerland and Bulgaria, where they were cut off from direct communication with other neutral powers. The Department of External Affairs and de Valera expressed their concern over the frequent use of the Northumberland Road transmitter in 1940 and 1941. Finally in 1942 de Valera and Joe Walshe, the Department's Secretary, requested Hempel to make no further use of it. Later Hempel was asked to hand it over altogether until the war was over and it was quietly placed in the vaults of the Munster and Leinster Bank in Dublin. Here again de Valera's resistance to German pressure was successful and his explanations for the lack of co-operation with regard to requests of this order were unhesitatingly accepted by the Germans. There was an epilogue to the transmitter story. In February 1944 the British and Americans presented separate notes in which they asked for the German and Japanese legations to be closed down—on the old grounds of alleged spying. The Americans did not know about the fate of the transmitter and stressed the issue; the British, who did, had chosen not to inform them. And this put the American minister and his government in a somewhat absurd position. De Valera had the appropriate answer once again, this time countering Anglo-American rather than German pressure.

It was from November 1940 that the British threat to neut-

rality appeared to mount acutely. Churchill in a famous
speech in the Commons on 5 November referred to the fact
that the cause of the free world, and the interests of Britain,
were seriously hindered by their navy being unable to use the
Irish ports against German submarines operating in the Atlantic. In that month too Franklin D. Roosevelt was elected for
his third term as President of the United States. To be re-
elected he had to secure the Irish vote, which normally, of
course, was by and large Democratic. It was quite clear that
Roosevelt wanted America to enter the war alongside Britain
—certainly after the fall of France. But the forces of isola-
tionism were still quite powerful. Many Irishmen in the States
not only wanted a neutral America; they also resisted any infringement of Irish neutrality, which might follow from
American action. David Gray, the American minister in
Dublin, was related to Roosevelt. In the summer of 1940 he
had strongly supported Irish requests for transport to their
army of rifles and ammunition. He had also favoured the
Irish purchase of freight ships from United States stocks. He
agreed with Churchill that an all-Ireland council should be
set up to secure unity of military policy between the northern
and southern governments; and initially he blamed the North
for the failure of this proposal. In fact during his first months
in Dublin he was rather in favour of de Valera. But he soon
changed his views very drastically. In changing them he made
the very big mistake of allowing his social connections to influence his political judgements. Gray gradually had become
attached to the hunting, fishing and shooting groups. This
had been his world in the United States, but he found it more
easily come by in Dublin. He had very little natural understanding of how other Irishmen, influenced by their history,
might feel. He went from one extreme to the other—a mistake
that Maffey, the British representative, did not make. Some
years later Maffey (later Lord Rugby), when he was leaving Ireland after the peculiar circumstances of Ireland's leaving the Commonwealth in 1948, paid special tribute at Dublin
airport to de Valera—because, as he said, 'we were both able

to look each other in the eye, and to believe what the other said'. Maffey had never left de Valera under any misunderstanding that, when it became vitally necessary for British interests, his country would take the required steps to invade and occupy Southern Ireland. Maffey also believed de Valera, when the Irish leader said that the Irish would oppose any attempt by the British to interfere with their neutrality. Maffey accepted de Valera's professions in respect of Irish neutrality, and de Valera accepted Maffey's word.

It was never quite clear what the British really wanted— at least it was not at all clear then. It is now known that the Ministry of Labour, Ernest Bevin, and the civil servants in the Ministry of Agriculture, along with the recruitment agencies of the air force and the army, saw no reason, as far as they were concerned, to fear or to reject Irish neutrality. Ireland had passed no foreign enlistment act, and Irish emigrant labour was of considerable assistance to the British war effort.

Irish civil servants in the Department of Finance, which was the principal department in Ireland, were never pro-German; many had, in fact, been trained by the British whom they respected, and there was constant communication between the Treasury and Merrion Street. The Irish intelligence service, too, maintained close connections throughout the war with their British counterparts. It was known that de Valera personally favoured the survival of democracy in Europe. It was equally known that he distrusted British and American policies, where neutral Irish interests might be concerned. But the same language applied as much to the Germans as to the British and the Americans. Still, despite the circumstances of personal trust between the Irish Taoiseach and the opposing diplomats, there were a number of dramatic moments, with Maffey and Hempel interviewing de Valera at all times of the day and night.

After the Russo-German war started on 22 June 1941 the conditions of public opinion in Ireland were more favourable than they had been regarding the neutral stand.

There were few Irishmen who could accept Stalinist Russia as the exponent of a new democratic or liberal world. When the United States joined in, in December 1941, American troops openly entered Northern Ireland. In the previous twelve months their engineers had already been engaged in the construction and development of naval and military bases in the North; and indeed after January 1942, Northern Ireland was to be employed as a training base for American, as well as British troops, preparing for the invasion of Europe. De Valera protested against this particular American occupation of Irish territory; he also expressed sympathy with what America had meant to Ireland in the past, while objecting to the apparent alignment of Britain and America on Irish soil. Here he pleased none of the western powers entirely, but at the same time he did not gravely offend any one of them.

December 1941 was in fact the critical turning point, but no one knew it at the time—except possibly Churchill who knew that Britain could never win a war on the continent without getting American troops over. As far as Ireland was concerned, this December was also a turning point. Why? No one, of course, then knew that.

The main reason was that Captain Goertz had been arrested on 27 November. The I.R.A. leaders had had their odd divisions in the Dublin mountains, when Goertz's friend, Hayes, the I.R.A. chief of staff, was caught and tortured by other I.R.A. men (from the North) before escaping into the safe arms of the police. These internal events virtually ended the effectively active role of the I.R.A. in international affairs, though their German friends could not have known that at the time. General O'Duffy was still around offering his services to the German Legation. There were one or two I.R.A radio operators, though by this stage it was not at all clear whom they hoped to serve. The spy game was virtually over, as far as Ireland was concerned.

From December 1941 to June 1944 the picture of Irish neutrality changes. There was, in fact, no longer any real danger of German invasion, though it was only in January 1943 that the project of landing a small group of Abwehr specialists was finally abandoned. This particular operation was connected in German eyes with Frank Ryan, once again, and with the Irish Legation in Madrid, along with whatever remained of the I.R.A. Nothing came from these schemes. In terms of great power politics future threats came only from Britain and America.

When America entered the war, Churchill sent a typically personal telegram to de Valera, in which he said that 'it was now or never for Orange and Green to unite'. His object was to bring Ireland into the war, and, at the same time, to achieve a basis for Irish unification—bringing him back to his old special romance of Home Rule and Ireland within the United Kingdom. And he proposed a meeting between himself and de Valera. This was sedulously avoided. He then thought the American card would be the trump to play. And in fact the real pressure against Irish neutrality was to come subsequently from the United States. Before 1942 there had been a good deal of British press talk about German spies in Ireland, dating especially from Churchill's speech of November 1940. All this gossip was proved to be false. Few informed people in British military, naval or civil service ministries had taken the reports seriously. But Roosevelt was different. The Americans, once they were in the war, wanted all their friends to hoist the same flag. So they applied more strenuous pressure on Ireland as the war continued. Churchill went on making his loud noises. It was only in 1942 that the war really hit Ireland, economically speaking. Churchill and Roosevelt had agreed on this kind of pressure, though they never pushed it too far. Even earlier, in March 1941, Frank Aiken (then Minister for the co-ordination of defence) had found it difficult to secure any sympathetic hearing from the American administration for Irish require-ments in respect of arms, ships and food. Roosevelt had obviously very little sympathy for de Valera's policy or for Irish neutrality. His attitude persisted, and he would seem to

B

have become even more personally involved than Churchill did (though with less excuse). He not only lost his temper with Aiken in April 1941, but also completely followed his relative David Gray's advice in connection with American policy towards Ireland right up to 1944 and 1945. Still the President was held in some check by the influence of many Irish Democrats and important members of the Catholic hierarchy in the United States.

A few months before the Anglo-American invasion of Europe on 6 June 1944, drastic measures were taken to cut off all communications stretching from the United Kingdom and Southern Ireland and to the continent. But by this time the real difficulties of neutrality were over. In any event they were completely removed by the success of the invasion. Nonetheless some apparently moral but in effect political issues were now to be raised by the British and the Americans. De Valera, for example, was asked to guarantee that he would hand over 'war criminals' to the jurisdiction of Anglo-American courts operating in Germany. Once again he had his answer ready. He did not specifically refuse to hand over anyone, but insisted that this did not preclude the exercise of the traditional right of asylum, where charity or the interests of the state applied. It was not easy for the British or the Americans to fault him on this reply.

The war ended in May 1945.

Neutrality seems to have been maintained on the lines laid down at the start. The law of neutrality involved reciprocity and impartiality. It was impossible to be reciprocal and impartial all the time, but de Valera did manage to uphold the principles involved—even though in practice Britain and America may have benefited more than Germany—in respect, for instance, of the passage of non-operational flights across Irish territory via Lough Erne, the internment of so-called ship-wrecked sailors, and the failure to introduce a foreign enlistment act. There were other thorny problems : when and how to 'black-out' and whether to sail Irish ships in British controlled convoys. The answers were found and at least they proved acceptable to the neutral state and the clamorous belligerents. Dublin was bombed in error by a German plane in May 1941 but, however distressing for the victims, this incident passed safely.

CONCLUSION

Certain conclusions follow from the story as it has now unrolled itself. The most important points are:

(a) The persistence with which de Valera kept the lines open to all interested parties—the Germans and the British through Hempel and Maffey, the Americans through Robert Brennan, and the Vatican through Kiernan—and thus paved the way for smooth communications in the event of every crisis.

(b) The fact that Ireland was fortunate in having two foreign diplomats of friendly disposition, Hempel and Maffey, each of whom ignored propaganda statements about Ireland and relied upon their personal knowledge of this country and its political leadership.

(c) The balance and common sense of Hempel who realized in particular the danger of adventuresome contact with the I.R.A. He also appreciated the danger of reporting fully back to Berlin on all the various small compliances with Anglo-American requests which might otherwise have been used to justify German retaliation between 1940 and 1945.

(d) The skill of de Valera in convincing all parties that he would oppose by force the first power which tried to interfere with Irish neutrality.

(e) The good fortune that the occupation of Irish territory never really became absolutely vital or was thought to become vital to the security of any of the belligerents. The advantages to be derived from any attempted occupation were not greater than the costs, moral and military, involved in such an operation.

(f) The secrecy within which de Valera shrouded his ultimate intentions and wishes, as a result of which all the parties primarily interested interpreted his statements according to their desires and in a sense favourable to themselves. De Valera in fact appears never to have told anyone, even in his cabinet, everything that was in his mind.

(g) The fact that the developments of the European military situation swung the main centre of the war from western to eastern Europe as from the end of 1941.

(h) The fact that partition made it possible for Britain to be indifferent to the existence of a relatively unarmed, weak and neutral Ireland, an attitude which would have been speedily abandoned if the entry to the Mersey and the Clyde channels had not been protected from the base at Derry.

(i) The successful balancing by Irish diplomacy of German against British, and British against German moves, between 1940 and 1944.

(j) The success of the Irish Minister in Washington, Robert Brennan, in controlling the reactions of Irish-American opinion through the war.

(k) The comparative weakness in 1940 of the air-arm, which made it impossible for the Luftwaffe to take a step which, in Hitler's opinion, could have decided the war.

(l)   The British discovery of radar which reduced the threat of German submarine warfare and made occupation of the Irish ports unnecessary.

(m)   The relative success of the economic policies pursued by the Irish government.

This was the combination of various factors which rendered neutrality possible. Some of these were technical and scientific in origin but most of them were the fruit of human skill.

The Irish Economy during the War

JAMES F. MEENAN

The outbreak of war in September 1939 found the Irish economy, and Irish economic policies, in a state of transition. The 1930s, it will be remembered, were a decade of world depression and of falling prices. This was intensified in the case of Irish agriculture by the penal duties imposed by the British government on our products entering the United Kingdom. It was offset to some extent by the vigorous encouragement of manufacturing industry. The Anglo-Irish Trade Agreement of April 1938 ended the economic war and opened the British market again. If the peace of Europe had been preserved, it would have been possible to look forward to a fruitful period in which a reviving agricultural export trade would have assisted the growth of industries which, at that early stage of their development, would have depended largely on the prosperity of the home market. The chances of this recovery and growth were destroyed by the outbreak of war. No time was available in which agriculture could have been restored.

So much might have been said by an observer in the autumn of 1939. But almost certainly he would have consoled himself with memories of what had happened in what was then called the Great War. In 1939 that war was only 21 years back in history. A person then still in vigorous middle-age might well have served throughout the 1914-18 war in one capacity or another. Such a person, were he an Irishman, would have recalled that in those years there had been a ready market for everything that Irish farmers could produce. The prices of all foodstuffs had steadily advanced throughout the war years to their peak in 1920. This had made, paradoxically enough, the last seven years of the Union with Great Britain the most prosperous years that had been experienced in modern Irish history. Prosperity had been diffused throughout the entire country, dominated as it then was by the fortunes of agriculture.

But the Second War was quite a different war from the First. It posed problems which were quite different from those of twenty-five years earlier. The first and essential difference of course was that in 1939 this country was an independent state, with a government that with the full agreement of its people was committed to a policy of neutrality. Therefore no precedents nor lessons could be drawn from the experiences of the First War in which Ireland was still a part of the United Kingdom. All the way down in the business of government, ministers and civil servants had to grope their way through the fog of war.

Neutrality and its maintenance was then the point of departure for all policy, economic as well as political. But it is still almost impossible for commentators to estimate what exactly neutrality meant, how far it implied complete dis-severance from the belligerents, how far it was in fact subtly attuned to half-understandings with them.

Let me give one example—an incident which, so far as I know, was not the subject of debate at the time nor later. It is like the tip of an ice-berg. One can see what is above the surface and is in full view. One can only guess at what is unseen.

At the time of the Munich crisis, in September 1938, the Currency Commission, which looked after the backing of our currency until the present Central Bank opened its doors in 1943, sold some two and a half million pounds worth of its

sterling securities and bought gold. This was indeed a very
provident thing to do. All the other countries that intended
to remain neutral did much the same at that time. If Great
Britain was going to war, it would obviously be better to hold
gold rather than sterling from the point of view of being able
to buy supplies from countries such as the United States. The
British, however, might not be expected to see things in that
light; and in fact some comment was passed on the Commission's action in the British financial press. Now the really
interesting thing is that in 1939—when the world was clearly
sliding towards war after the German annexation of Czechoslovakia in March—the Currency Commission held on to its
sterling and bought no more gold. To an outsider it does
rather look as if a gentleman's agreement had been reached
on the basis that if Ireland continued to hold sterling, the
British government would do its best to assure some level of
supplies. But, of course, this may be quite wrong.

At any rate, here the country was in 1939, trying to maintain a neutrality for which there was no precedent, trying
to work out a quite new relationship with one of the major
belligerents—and it was that belligerent that commanded the
seas and could determine the volume of supplies to Ireland.

A look at the trade returns does not suggest that in 1939,
before or after the declaration of war, was there any great
attempt to stockpile essential raw materials, such as petrol,
coal or fertilizers. The imports for 1939 are much the same
as those for 1938 which in its turn, being the year of the
Trade Agreement and therefore a year of optimism, was
rather up on 1937. But there was no great expansion of
purchases. This may well have been due to the shortage of
storage space, storage space which had never been needed
in peace time and did not appear to receive much attention
at the time. It may well have been due also to the course
that the war took in its early months. Many people, not
alone in this country, were persuaded that the Second World
War would be a continuation of the First in its strategy as
well as in everything else; and that there would be a stable

front in Flanders as there had been in the well-remembered days of 1916 and 1917. That did in fact happen until May 1940. Until then, it was permissible to believe that supplies could be readily obtained across seas still relatively undisputed by Nazi Germany.

As things developed, the maintenance of supplies at whatever level and however intermittently turned out to be the main theme of Irish neutrality. At the outbreak of war, a new department was set up—of Supplies, which was headed by Mr Seán Lemass who temporarily abandoned Industry and Commerce to Mr Seán MacEntee. Rationing was soon introduced and soon every citizen was acquainted with the signature of Mr John Leydon, who was secretary of the new department. The availability of supplies of anything depended on many matters which were outside the control of Mr Lemass. They depended increasingly, as the war wore on, on the degree of cordiality between Ireland and the major allies. Even if, however, the United Kingdom and the United States were agreed on furnishing supplies—and it was a minor paradox of the war that relations with the British improved as relations with the United States went from bad to worse—they were not always able to get supplies across the Atlantic. Throughout all vicissitudes, Mr Lemass never hesitated to prepare everybody for the worst. This was superlatively good public relations. The worst never did quite come to the worst; and everybody put up with a lot because they had been prepared to have to put up with so much more. In those years, Mr Lemass consistently concealed the strength of his hand.

But when one speaks of supplies coming in, the reference is only to the most essential supplies. For a very wide range of the new industries, the flow of raw materials was almost completely cut off. This entailed a steep fall in industrial production and employment. Some industries indeed were able to maintain, even to expand, production. The good humour of British and American forces in the Six Counties, for example, depended to a large extent on the maintenance of supplies of stout; and there was at least one occasion when an intimation that these supplies could not be guaranteed on account of lack of coal for the trains to convey them northwards produced coal supplies with remarkable celerity. But some forms of employment—motor-car assembly, soap and candle making for example—fell to less than half their pre-war activity; and there were very few industries indeed that were not affected by the shortage of raw materials.

The inevitable result was the turning off of labour. In the circumstances of the time, this did not mean unemployment. The demand for labour in Great Britain, quite apart from the lure of the fighting services, saw to it that emigration rose steadily, as men and women left their narrowing opportunities of work here for the attractive terms of work across the water. By 1942 it was necessary to control emigration and to attempt, with some measure of success, to forbid the emigration of agricultural workers who were needed for the harvests. Industrial workers, you will notice, were almost always allowed to go freely. Nevertheless it is remarkable that all this war-induced emigration did not greatly affect the level of population. The census of 1946 showed a fall in total population of only thirteen thousand as compared with 1936. What did matter was the replacement of young adults, who emigrated in large numbers, with an increased number of small children; but that is another matter.

As had happened twenty-five years before, the war brought a notable extension of tillage. For some years before the war, it had been government policy to encourage wheat-growing. This was now given a fresh impetus; and compulsory tillage orders, which were in force throughout the war, brought the tillage area to the highest point reported for decades.

But agriculture did not experience anything like the sustained prosperity of the First World War. There were a number of reasons for that. There was, in the first place, the sheer bad luck of a severe outbreak of foot-and-mouth disease in 1941 which reduced stocks at a vitally important juncture. More generally, farms were still run down after the losses of the depression and the economic war; and there had not been enough time to lay the foundations of recovery.

A third reason was to be only too prophetic of what lay ahead after the war was over. In 1939-45 much of the British war effort was directed by men who had experience at first hand of what had happened in the First World War. They knew what mistakes had to be avoided. They were also concerned—and this had not been the case in the First World War—to safeguard British agriculture. This was reflected in the British prices for farm products. They were carefully controlled: they were not allowed to climb the peaks that had been so profitable to Irish farmers in the First World War.

On the contrary, in 1944 it was noted that the prices offered by the British Ministry of Food were actually lower than pre-war prices. They were lower than current prices in Ireland. The plea was that policy aimed at maintaining the pre-war relationship between the prices paid to Irish and to dominion suppliers of the British market. Whatever may be thought of the defensibility of this outlook, it did mean that there was remarkably little money to be made out of selling food to Great Britain.

This was not at all appreciated at the time. Then, the picture was rather of a neutral country making easy money out of the difficulties of others. You will find this opinion expressed, forcibly and grotesquely, in the highest quarters. Take for example, Sir Winston Churchill's books on the Second World War which include a selection from the directives with which he used stimulate his colleagues. Here is one, dated 1 December 1941 and addressed by him to the Chancellor of the Exchequer:

> The straits to which we are being reduced by Irish action compel a reconsideration of the subsidies [to Ireland]. It can hardly be argued that we can go on paying them to our last gasp. . . Pray let me know how these subsidies could be terminated and what retaliatory measures could be taken in the financial sphere by the

Irish, observing that we are not afraid of their cutting off their food, as it would save us the enormous mass of fertilizers and feeding-stuffs we have to carry into Ireland through the de Valera-aided German blockade.

It will help to look at that more closely. There were subsidies on Irish farm produce going into Great Britain. They were paid by the Irish government, not the British. As for fertilizers, the returns show the imports going in this way. In the peace-time year of 1938, there were 80,000 tons of phosphate brought in. The figure was 89,000 tons in 1939 and 74,000 tons in 1940. In 1941, the year in which Churchill wrote, there were 7,000 tons brought in and in 1942 none at all. The import of fertilizers was not to regain the pre-war levels for years to come.

As for feeding-stuffs: in 1938, some 7,000,000 hundredweight of maize had been imported. The figure in 1939 was 8,000,000, in 1940 it was less than 6,000,000. There was less than 1,000,000 tons brought in during 1941 and there was none at all in 1942, 1943 and 1944.

These figures are not brought in to pursue an old quarrel. Rather they illustrate the difficulties of agriculture and of the farming community during the war years. Prices for their produce did not increase in any degree comparable to the rise in the general price level. They were obliged to expand production with greatly reduced supplies of fertilizers and feeding-stuffs. To be sure, the input of fertilizers had been scandalously low even in peace time; but the conditions of war time meant that for the moment the fertility of the land was being undermined.

We therefore got the remarkable result that even in the seemingly favourable conditions of war time, the value of exports remained far below the level of the pre-depression years. The best year for exports, in money terms, was 1945, when £35 million of produce was sent out. But that was well below the £47 million of produce sent out in 1929—and the pounds were not so good. In terms of volume, exports during the war were rather less than half what they had been fifteen years before.

Nevertheless, if the export position was bad, the import position was worse still. The simple non-availability of finished goods and raw materials was reflected in a shrinking bill for imports. In 1941 and again in 1943 and 1944 we actually exported more than we imported and had a surplus on the balance of visible trade. This, as you will have seen, was not due to any achievement of exporting more—it was simply the result of importing less because we had to go without.

Financially, of course, this had its advantages. The external assets, which had been drawn down to some extent during the 1930s, were replenished. This was rather artificial because the recovery came only from a species of forced saving; and it was plain that, as soon as goods were available again, assets would be drawn down—as indeed proved to be the case in 1947 and later. But observers during the war noted the financial buoyancy of the country. This considerably helped financing during the war. As late as 1943, nine tenths of government expenditure was met out of current revenue. It was very rightly said at the time that Ireland was a great deal sounder financially than it was economically.

These were years in which employment was difficult to retain as raw materials grew more scarce. They were also years in which the standard of living fell even for those who were fortunate enough to keep their jobs. The cost of living index which was calculated on the basis of the price level of July 1914 being equal to 100 had been 173 in 1938. By 1943 it had risen to 284—and at that time it was only on the threshold of really sharp annual advances. But although prices went up, wages and salaries were held down by the emergency order which restricted increases. The intention of the standstill order was to avoid the unchecked inflation which would have resulted from an increase in money incomes when goods were simply not available. That disaster was avoided; but only at the cost of considerable hardship.

One can believe now that it was better to prevent inflation in this choice of evils—but the strain meant that post-war revisions in wages and salaries were thorough-going by way of reaction.

Added to all this was the hardship of scarcity of ordinary goods—although in many cases rationing alleviated the worst consequences. From an early stage in the war sugar, tea and fuel were rationed. In 1942 bread and clothing were added. A really serious crisis would have resulted had it ever come to pass that the bread ration could not be honoured—but that never quite happened. Petrol for private motoring finally went out in the same year of 1942. Coal, for households, became rarer than diamonds, and people accustomed themselves, not always willingly, to the provision of war-time turf. A little later, gas and electricity were rationed. It gives the reader a nostalgic jab to find that throughout the summer of 1944, the tram service in Dublin was suspended. By that time also, the railway system was a ghost of its peace-time self. There were two passenger trains to Cork each week. The duration of the voyage might be anything from eight to twelve hours. This was at first attributed to the poor quality of the fuel; later it was thought that the fuel was not being handled by railwaymen as efficiently as it might have been. To sum up the supply situation—by 1943 the community had 25 per cent of its normal requirements of tea, 20 per cent of its requirements of petrol, less than 15 per cent of its paraffin, 16 per cent of its gas coal, no domestic coal whatever and 22 per cent of its textiles.

Thus the shortage of raw materials affected every part of national life. In agriculture, it restricted production and affected the crop yields. In manufacturing industry, the shortages meant that many factories had to close down altogether; and many others had to adjust themselves as best they could. In one way or another, the effect was to swell the emigration to England which might have been expected to increase even if economic activity could have been maintained at a higher level. This emigration came from temporary causes; but it was not to prove temporary. It was not reversed when raw materials became available again after the war. Many of the emigrants remained in England, building up Irish communities there which were to be magnets for fresh emigration in the 1950s.

These were the most obvious results. Less apparent but at least as important was the strain which the war, and the impossibility of maintenance, placed on machinery and productive equipment of all kinds. Here the supreme example was the land itself—much more than usual was taken out while the input of fertilizer was heavily reduced. Another example, which was to surface after the war, was provided by the railways. Even before the war began, the state of rolling stock and of the permanent way was highly unsatisfactory over wide areas. The passage of seven years in which it was almost impossible to make replacements made a bad situation all but intolerable. In one way or another, the same situation obtained throughout most of manufacturing industry. Plant became increasingly obsolete and, in all cases, overworked.

All this was a more prolonged crisis than may appear today. One thinks of the war of course as starting in 1939 and ending in 1945. But these shortages I have described did not cease when hostilities ended. They continued for a long time afterwards—well into 1947 and in some cases into 1948 and even 1949.

It is rather this post-war period that, in retrospect, seems to have provided the greatest test of government. If things went short during the war itself, it was common sense to reflect that nothing could be safe in war time. The question then was rather the subjective one of whether the government appeared to be doing all it could within the limits of its freedom of action. The war-time government stood that test very well. But once the strain of the war was over, it was very hard to see why the world could not get back to the conditions of 1939 without delay. To look after the economy of this country in 1946 and 1947 must in many ways have been a much more difficult task than dealing with the exigencies of the war.

Matters may be summed up—in so far as economic issues are concerned—by saying that the country survived the war —in much the same sense as the Abbé Sieyès survived the French Revolution. It did not, except in an artificial and temporary sense, add to its wealth. On the contrary, its wealth was diminished by the war. But the economy just managed to keep going; and above all, the policy of neutrality was not prejudiced by economic weakness. It was a severe test for an immature economy that was caught in a state of transition by the outbreak of war. Nevertheless, the country emerged with a reasonably sound currency, with maintained external assets and with a public debt that was still manageable. All these things were useful achievements; the true gain was the access of confidence which came from the sense of a severe test that had been successfully met.

Irish Defence Policy, 1938-51

G. A. HAYES-MCCOY

The defence policy of Mr de Valera's government during the Second World War was inspired by a determination to preserve the neutrality of the state. It was a policy deliberately adopted and steadfastly pursued. It reflected the wishes, as declared by their parliamentary representatives and as shown by their actions, of the majority of the citizens, and it met with success.

It had of course been suggested even before the war began that the real defences of Ireland were not those which might be put up by her people—the defences, that is, on which the government declared itself to rely—but rather the British navy, and the fact that Ireland is geographically remote from central Europe. It would be quite wrong—thirty years after the event—to minimize the effect which another people's battleships and aeroplanes and the all-important matter of distance had on the situation. And retrospection prompts something more. Nobody seems to have thought thirty years ago that the horrid fact of partition made things easier for us; indeed Mr de Valera said in 1939 that it would have been ten times easier to draw up a defence scheme for Ireland if the island was not partitioned and if the Six Counties were included with the Twenty-Six in an independent state. One may well suggest now that such a state, if it had existed, might not have been quite so enthusiastic about Irish neutrality. And it goes without saying that Britain would have found it much harder to refrain from an infringement of that neutrality if she had been excluded from the Six Counties of Northern Ireland, as she was excluded from the remaining Twenty-Six.

The prospect of a European war increased notably in the spring and summer of 1939. The new Germany, Hitler's Germany, which had occupied the Rhineland in 1936 and had annexed Austria and begun the dismemberment of Czechoslovakia in 1938, moved troops into Prague in March. Mussolini, modern Europe's original dictator, led Italy closer to a German alliance. The Netherlands and Belgium, uneasily placed on the western border of Germany, held their breath. Russia, the enigma, watched, negotiated—and watched again.

In the same fateful month of March, Poland, although she lay between Hitler's hammer and Stalin's anvil, boasted that Czechoslovakia's fate would not be hers. Britain and France stiffened. Britain dropped her former policy of the appeasement of Hitler, guaranteed Poland against German aggression, and looked with mounting anxiety to the developing prospect of a return to some at least of the horrors of 1915-18. The war drums throbbed, and those who did not beat them watched their defences.

What did we do? What could we do? We had at the beginning of 1939 an army of 20,000 of all ranks—that is, a regular army of about 7,000 and a reserve of more than 12,000. More than 7,000 of these reservists were inadequately trained Volunteers—the parliamentary opposition called them Fianna Fáil Volunteers. We had never seriously contemplated using any of these soldiers in extended warfare. We had no source of war supplies within our shores and we were sadly deficient in much that was essential for the equipment of a modern army.

Since 1922, when the state was founded, many constitutional changes and one most significant change involving the government's authority within its own territory had taken place. The Irish Free State was born into the British Empire. The Conferences of 1926 and 1930, in which we took part, modified imperialism and led to the passing of the Statute of Westminster, which underlined the independence of the states—including ours—that were members of the British Commonwealth of Nations. The External Relations Act of 1936 and the new Irish Constitution of 1937 gave further evidence of our independent—indeed, our republican—status. In 1938 Mr de Valera's government made an important agreement—Winston Churchill called it 'lamentable and amazing'—with the British government of Mr Neville Chamberlain.

This agreement not only terminated the so-called economic war, which had embittered relations between the two countries since 1932, but also provided for the abandonment by Britain of rights which she had retained under the treaty of 1921—the right to station coast defence maintenance parties at Berehaven, Cork harbour and Lough Swilly in time of peace, and, in time of war, the right to such additional harbour and other facilities as might be required.

These provisions, and, in particular, the second of them— a vague, far-reaching provision, certain to be interpreted in war time to suit the stronger state, certain to provoke conflict if it was so interpreted—would, of themselves, rule out the possibility of Ireland's neutrality in a war in which Britain was involved. Their abandonment in 1938—almost on the eve of the Second World War—completely altered the Irish defence position and had, of course, most far-reaching results. Mr de Valera posed the question a year later: Why did the British government surrender the ports? His answer, in view of the tremendous issues involved, fell rather flat. He said that Chamberlain had probably balanced the pros and cons and had concluded that it was better not to continue to hold our ports against the opposition of the Irish people.[1]

1. *Dáil Éireann, Parliamentary Debates,* lxxiv, 716, 16 Feb. 1939.

Or was this really as flat as it sounds? If, in the end, and as a direct result of the agreement of 1938, Mr de Valera could practise neutrality, Britain—making do with bases in Northern Ireland, in particular, Derry, and moving her Atlantic convoy routes north after the fall of France—won her war.

But this is to anticipate. In the Dáil at the beginning of February 1939, seven months before the commencement of the war, the Fine Gael opposition moved for the setting up of a select committee to report on the failure of the government to provide protection for the people against the possibility of attack from the air.[2] Their spokesmen held that the army could not work out a defence plan because the government had no defence policy. Mr Aiken, who was at that time Minister for Defence, was placatory in his reply. He said nothing about policy, but spoke of air raid precautions, the danger of gas attacks, shelter trenches in back gardens, and the evacuation of children, the aged and invalids from Dublin —all, of course, in the event of war. The opposition motion was defeated. A week later, Mr Aiken had more to say. Moving a supplementary estimate for the army, he told the Dáil that the General Headquarters staff had drawn up plans in the light of the following facts—that the state had complete and internationally recognized sovereignty over all parts of the island outside the Six Counties of Northern Ireland; that only our elected representatives could commit us to war; that we had no existing commitments which would involve us in war; that it was not the policy of the government to attack any nation, but that it *was* the policy of the government to repel any attack which might be made on the territory of the state. There was no possibility of our being at war with Britain unless she attacked us. All this meant that, in the event of a European war, we should be neutral. In all probability, our only likely adversary would be a power that was at war with Britain and that might seek to make Irish territory a base from which to attack Britain.

2. *Ibid.*, lxxiv, 182 ff. 8 Feb. 1939.

In these circumstances the problem which faced the government and the Headquarters staff was how best, within the limits of our resources and in the shortest possible time, to secure an adequate defence force. It was proposed to increase the army to a maximum strength of 30,000 men, made up of a regular force of 8,000, a reserve of 5,000, and a Volunteer reserve of 17,000. It was also proposed to spend up to £5 million on weapons, equipment and warlike stores. The Minister painted a vivid—indeed, a highly coloured—picture of mobilized strength. He spoke of a leadership of experienced officers; a well-equipped and highly trained army that would include a 'striking force', garrisons for the harbour defence works, cycle squadrons and anti-aircraft artillery; an air force; a marine service including coast watching, patrol and minesweeping units; and an adequate air raid precautions service. He said that arrangements were being made to build an ammunition factory. If we wanted to be left in peace, if we wanted to be allowed to continue our economic and social development according to our wishes, we must be prepared to make sacrifices in the cause of defence. Only by doing so could we hope to confront a potential attacker with the deterrent of force.

This was the government view. The opposition was not quite so sanguine. Many people both inside and outside the Dáil doubted Ireland's ability to remain neutral, particularly 'to the tune of £5 million'. It was pointed out that some European countries which had been willing to spend not £5 million but £500 million on defence, had been unable to maintain neutrality, an observation which was soon to be given even more point by the progress of events. It was asked if we seriously believed that we could, with 30,000 riflemen, oppose a power which could reach us only by bursting through the British navy. In general, the Fine Gael opposition advocated the spending of money on the development of an air force rather than a ground army. They asked how we could remain neutral if Britain were at war and we continued to export foodstuffs to her. Some believed that our military preparations were needless, and that it would suffice to proclaim our neutrality and rely on moral force—as represented by the voices of Irishmen all over the world—to uphold it. Mr Dillon thought that we should declare ourselves for 'decency, tolerance and freedom' against 'the medieval barbarism of the dictators'.

The endless talk of those dying days of peace was not all the result of wishful thinking, or of party politics. Mr McGilligan asked searching questions. If we visualized meeting an attack from a continental power by a combined operation of Irish and British troops, was there to be unity of command? How would Northern Ireland figure in such an arrangement? Would it not be better to admit that we could not ourselves exploit the strategic value of Berehaven, Cork harbour and Lough Swilly and that, indeed—although in the matter of defence our road was parallel with the British road—we had no wish to do so; would it not be better to admit that and to make a new arrangement with the British for the defence of the ports?

These were shrewd questions—Britain, aware of the value of the ports for the protection of her convoys, would soon raise them; yet Mr Aiken's reply may be said to have been shrewder still. He said that the 'fellow on the opposite side' —he meant, of course, Hitler—must think twice before violating our neutrality, since such violation would automatically mean that our ports would be at Britain's disposal. Meanwhile, we were, as a neutral state, going to defend our own harbours.[3]

Mr de Valera, who, like Churchill, could select a phrase, said that we were 'for the first time facing this particular obligation of freedom, the obligation of trying to preserve it'. The leader of the opposition, Mr Cosgrave, was blunt; if we were going to be neutral, he said, we must be 'armed against all sides'.[4]

This was the position in the early summer of 1939. We

3. *Ibid.,* lxxiv, 765 ff., 16 Feb. 1939.
4. *Ibid.,* lxxiv, 724, 16 Feb. 1939.

were, Mr de Valera had told the world press,[5] 'determined to keep our nation out of war'. He said that, although we had no British commitments, we knew that, should an attack come from any other power, Britain must, in her own interest, 'help us to repel it'. Mr Aiken said that we could not have neutrality merely by wishing for it; or, as he put it, that there was 'no use in trying to substitute a wishbone for a backbone'.[6]

The moment when words alone might no longer suffice came in September. The Russo-German pact of the previous month had taken a world which thought itself wide-awake by surprise. On 1 September Hitler invaded Poland. On the 3rd Britain and France—Poland's allies—declared war on Germany. For the second time in the lives of most of us the lights went out. World War Two had begun.

Dáil Éireann resolved 'that a national emergency exists' and an Emergency Powers Act 'for securing the public safety and the preservation of the state in time of war' was speedily passed. The government was given authority to regulate supplies, fix prices, institute censorship, detain persons, and deal as best they could with what the opposition readily admitted as 'an unprecedented difficulty'. Army reservists were mobilized.[7]

Ominous things happened in the first few days. Troops occupied railway stations and other positions—the old-type troops, regulars, in a darker green than we know now, with long, ruddy brown leggings and squat, German-style helmets. Volunteers—soldiers of the part-time reserve Volunteer Force formed in 1934—appeared everywhere, their German-type uniforms a stilted reminder of Casement's brigade, and evidence too of our instinctive avoidance of things English.

5. Associated Press release, 20 Feb. 1939.

6. *Dáil Éireann, Parliamentary Debates,* lxxiv, 2318, 22 March 1939.

7. For the debate following the introduction of the Bill see *Dáil Éireann, Parliamentary Debates,* 2 Sept. 1939, cols. 19 ff. The Bill was passed through the Dáil and Senate on 2 and 3 September 1939. The army reserve was called up for permanent service on 1 September. The steps taken to implement this order are detailed in P. D. Kavanagh (ed.), *Irish Defence Forces Handbook,* Dublin 1968, 13.

On the first sad Sunday, in the pouring rain, an army plane flew out over the blacked-out mailboat as she left Dún Laoghaire—the 'Scotia' perhaps, soon to be lost at Dunkirk.

But the mood soon changed. Hitler, after he and Stalin had overrun Poland, stayed where he was. The period of the phoney war set in. Had the pattern of things altered? Had warfare lost something of its horror? With us, as with the people of other countries, hope revived. We soon began to demobilize, and had released 5,000 men—a quarter of our strength—from service with the colours by March 1940.

We had had, of course, an unpleasant reminder of the changelessness of Irish politics at Christmas, when members of the Irish Republican Army raided the magazine fort in the Phoenix Park and, surprising the small guard of the 7th (Dublin) Infantry Battalion—a reserve unit, made up largely of Volunteers—got away with over a million rounds of ammunition. The parliamentary opposition was caustic in its references to the raid : the government, it was said, was now faced with the kind of activity which they themselves had been guilty of some years before; was it wise to order more ammunition when we could not hold what we had? But there was no doubt that the action of the I.R.A. recoiled on itself. Practically all the stolen ammunition was soon recovered. An organization which could at a time of crisis call the state troops 'the enemy', and could operate against them, was shown up in what even the emotionally inclined realized were unattractive colours. Although I.R.A. activities more than once made the headlines and, more frequently still, caused anxiety in high places, the government was able to control the subversive element for the remainder of the war-time emergency. Numbers were interned.[8] And the raid had another result. It led to a necessary tightening of army discipline.

8. An estimate of the extent and significance of wartime I.R.A. activity is given in the reminiscences of Mr G. Boland, who was Minister for Justice at the time, in M. McInerney, 'Gerry Boland's Story', *The Irish Times*, 15–19 Oct. 1968.

1940 was our most anxious year. We saw that we might run short of supplies, and as Hitler, who was in undisputed possession of the initiative and who appeared to be invincible, seized Norway, overran Denmark, Belgium, Holland, Luxemburg—overran France (oh!—incredible feat!) the cold breath of fear touched us and our emergency became a reality. The Germans were in the Channel Islands and were preparing to attack the British mainland. It was rumoured (we now know that this was mere deception) that they were considering landing five or six divisions on our south coast.[9]

On 28 May, the day on which the Belgian army surrendered, and, incidentally, a German agent was arrested in Dublin, Mr de Valera announced a new Irish mobilization. The atmosphere of the Dáil changed. One can still feel the tension as Mr Cosgrave, followed by Mr Norton, echoed the Taoiseach's words: 'There is but one line of safety for us, to be ready to resist to the utmost whosoever may attack us.'[10] Our defence policy had not changed, but for most Irishmen neutrality ceased to be (the words are those of Mr McGilligan) 'some sort of a closed compartment in which people could hide'.[11]

As a matter of organization, our defence problem was twofold: to recruit and train as large an army as we could, and to equip and supply it. The authorized establishment for 1940 was for a regular force of 14,000 and a reserve, including Volunteers, of 12,000. We began recruiting for a far larger army in June. A new Defence Forces Bill, which passed through all its stages in two days, provided for enlistment for the duration of the emergency, for billeting and other contingencies, and

9. Operation Green. Cf. J. W. Blake, *Northern Ireland in the Second World War*, Belfast, 1956, 154 f; W. Ansel, *Hitler Confronts England*, 1960, 230 f. See also a notable article, Denis Ireland, 'In Time of the Breaking of Nations', *The Irish Times*, 3 Feb. 1968, in which he speaks of the general question of the defence of Ireland in the light of both Napoleon's and Hitler's confrontation of Britain.

10. *Dáil Éireann, Parliamentary Debates*, lxxx, 1169, 28 May 1940.

11. *Ibid.*, lxxix, 1564, 18 April 1940.

for the placing of the troops on active service.[12] A supplementary army estimate for £3 million was adopted in November. A new type of Irish soldier appeared—in new battalions, new batteries, new squadrons—infantry, artillery, cavalry, engineers, signals, ordnance, supply and transport, medical service, military police—a soldier in a new paler green uniform with a new British-type helmet. By Easter 1941, when these marching men, rank on rank, their long bayonets agleam in grey weather, paraded for the twenty-fifth anniversary of the 1916 Rising, it was plain that, in the midst of war—the Germans were soon to invade Russia; by the end of the year America was in—we were not defenceless. We had increased our Air Corps and had established a small Marine Service, and we had established a Local Security Force, one branch of which, made up of tens of thousands of patriotic enthusiasts, developed into the armed Local Defence Force. In all, although our actual figures were much less, we could soon begin to speak of an aggregate strength of 250,000 men.

The problem of the provision of war supplies remained, and Fine Gael spokesmen held that the government had been remiss in not attending to it earlier. Britain was our chief source of supply. In the early days we got some Bren guns, some Swedish Bofors AA guns and Landsverk armoured cars and some French Brandt mortars, and later we got American rifles, but our main armaments, which were light and less than adequate, were British.

The British too were our chief cause of anxiety. Sympathy for Germany, which was quite evident in the beginning, declined with German success. Sympathy for Britain increased, and there was throughout the war, and despite the fact that British recruiting advertisements were forbidden here, a very considerable Irish enlistment in the British forces. Before the collapse of France, Britain, although she took the

12. Defence Forces (Temporary Provisions) (No. 2) Bill, 1940. For its provisions and for the debate see *Dáil Éireann, Parliamentary Debates*, lxxx, 1522 f., 5 June 1940. For the new category of soldier, the Emergency Durationist, created by the Amendment, and for the organization of the army, 1940–45 see P. D. Kavanagh (ed.), *op. cit.*, 13 f.

precaution of covertly patrolling our coast,[13] had been scrupul-
ous in her recognition of our neutrality. So had Germany.
What would Britain do now that her back was to the wall?
In fact, she asked us to permit the entry of her troops to fore-
stall a possible German invasion, and when we refused that,
refused her the use of our ports and rejected her proposal for
a joint defence council,[14] she deployed her 53rd Division
along the Border, held a Royal Marine brigade at Milford
Haven and planned to fall on Dublin, Collinstown and Bal-
donnel should the Germans appear.[15] Mr de Valera said that
any British attempt to bring pressure to bear on us would
lead to bloodshed. Later on, when the proposal to extend
British conscription to Northern Ireland was revived, he led
a united Dáil in condemning what he suggested would be—
in its implication for the Nationalist minority—a wanton out-
rage. Mr Churchill, displaying statesmanlike restraint, vetoed
the conscription proposal.

Mr de Valera's handling of this dangerous and unprecedented situation must, in retrospect, be recognized as extra-
ordinarily skilful, all the more so because the Irish state was
an infant one. Granted that, more than anything else, we
owed our escape from involvement to our isolation—our
geographical isolation, and the separateness and homogeneity
which resulted from our being cut away from Northern Ireland,
and which so greatly favoured united action on our part;
granted these things, the course of neutrality was not easy.
Yet the government held to it most faithfully. Our censorship
was run on pedantic lines. We could claim that, formally,
we treated the belligerents alike. We scotched the allegation
that we had given supplies to German submarines by saying

13. Cf. W. R. Fell, *The Sea our Shield*, London 1966, 20–30.
14. The British Cabinet Papers recently released for public inspection
suggest that Mr de Valera's government was more anxious in 1938 for Anglo-
Irish defence co-operation than either Mr de Valera or his Ministers were
willing, in the following year, to admit in the Dáil. Fine Gael spokesmen
advocated such co-operation, but the government repeatedly parried questions
concerning it.
15. J. W. Blake, *op. cit.*, 155–60.

that it was a lie, and that Britain knew that it was a lie.
When bombs were dropped on Dublin in May 1941, we
immediately protested to Germany. Added to this, there was
the adroit handling of the domestic situation. On the one
hand, the I.R.A. was checked—so well checked that Germany
made no serious attempt to make use of it—yet, on the other,
advantage was taken of every occasion that offered to decry
partition. This was often, perhaps, a matter of propaganda,
and if it was it has had no lasting results, but it encouraged
the nationalist feeling which was an essential ingredient of
our war-time solidarity.

Gradually, the situation became easier, although the worst
shock that the public was aware of followed the landing of
United States troops in Northern Ireland in 1942, part of
the great build-up of allied forces which led eventually to the
invasion of Normandy in 1944. The government protested
at the presence of these troops in the North and it was erron-
eously thought for a moment in 1944 that our neutrality
might be violated, not by Britain or Germany, but by our
traditional friends. The crisis passed, and as the war rolled
backwards towards Germany we became complacent. Our
warlike stores increased, because Britain, as soon as she had
built up her own stocks and saw that we really meant to
defend ourselves, sold us more weapons and ammunition, but
recruiting fell off after 1943.

The only test of an army is combat. The war ended in
Europe in May 1945 and our troops were still untried. But
they had been trained in what were, for the purpose, not
inappropriate circumstances. The manoeuvres of autumn
1942, in which two complete divisions took part, were the
state's largest military exercise. We showed that we had a
competent, although inadequately armed, striking force. This,
for an army which had hitherto been vaguely considered
against a receding background of guerrilla—and civil—war
as a 'trained nucleus' maintained for an unspecified purpose,
was a satisfactory disclosure, and one hopes that it was an
inspiring one.

We had administered our army throughout the emergency, and since 1923, on a series of annual Defence Forces Acts; and when a permanent Act was eventually passed in 1954 it produced no statement regarding future defence policy. An inter-party conference which was provided for in 1940 to discuss defence measures soon lapsed, and nothing—unfortunately—has been heard of it since the war. When the army of the emergency stood down, United Nations service was far in the future, but one feels that our soldiers could not have served the cause of peace as they have done with such outstanding success in recent years if the army to which they belong had done less well in the midst of worldwide warfare.

Ulster During the War and After

DAVID KENNEDY

The 1930s were bleak years for Northern Ireland, years of high unemployment and sectarian riots. Thirty-seven per cent of Belfast's population lived in overcrowded or unfit houses and the rates of infant and maternal mortality were the highest in the United Kingdom.[1] Fifty per cent of all houses in Co. Fermanagh were 'unfit for human habitation'.[2] Resentment and frustration drove young Nationalists into the I.R.A. while unemployed Unionists eked out the dole with mobilization grants from the B-Specials. Yet in 1938 Lord Craigavon fought and won his last general election, wiping out a formidable challenge from the Progressive Unionists, and, like an expert illusionist, distracting attention from 100,000 unemployed[3] at home by asking the electorate to focus their eyes on the goings-on in London where British cabinet ministers were negotiating with the government of Éire.

Mr de Valera had given Lord Craigavon his cue by announcing that partition would be discussed in these negotiations. There is no evidence that the discussion amounted to more than an occupation of old positions. Éire was relieved of the obligation to pay the land annuities and Lord Craigavon used this as a lever to prise financial benefits from Britain. Northern Ireland had always been permitted to retain

1. R. J. Lawrence, *The Government of Northern Ireland*, Oxford 1965, 136.
2. J. M. Mogey, *Rural life in Northern Ireland*, Oxford 1947. 33, 207.
3. J. W. Blake, *Northern Ireland in the Second World War*, H.M.S.O. Belfast 1956, 537.

the land annuities. It was now agreed that agricultural subsidies granted in Great Britain might also be granted in Northern Ireland and the cost would be borne by the British Exchequer. Furthermore, it was agreed that any deficit in the Stormont Budget would be made good by the British Treasury provided that such deficit was not the result of lower taxation or higher social welfare than in Britain.[4] This principle of parity, parity of taxation and parity of social services, saved Northern Ireland from impending bankruptcy.

By this time the benefits of rearmament were being felt in Northern Ireland. The shipyard, the new aircraft factory, the engineering works, the clothing factories were sharing the surplus contracts available after the claims of other distressed areas such as Tyneside and South Wales had been met. When war broke out in September 1939 even the issue of gas masks, identity cards and ration books could not dispel the feelings of relief that came with the regular weekly pay-packet. For the moment the terrors of war were far off.

When the Conscription Act was passed in England, Lord Craigavon proposed that it be applied to Northern Ireland. The Catholic bishops of the Province thought that 'any attempt to impose conscription would be disastrous' and that their people would be roused to 'indignation and resistance'.[5] The proposal was dropped, to be re-opened in 1941 when the Home Secretary asked for the views of the Northern government. The Unionist Council when consulted gave the Prime Minister support, not directly for conscription, but for 'any action which he and his colleagues might decide to take'. The Catholic hierarchy reiterated their objections; the Nationalists pledged themselves to resist conscription by 'the most effective means at their disposal'; the Northern Ireland Labour Party demanded a plebiscite.[6]

4. *Ulster Year Book* 1938, H.M.S.O. Belfast, p. iv.
5. See *The Irish Catholic Directory and Almanac*, 1940, Statement of bishops of N. Ireland, 30 Apr. 1939.
6. Blake, *op. cit.*, 196–7.

No doubt the representations made in London by the United States Ambassador and by the Prime Minister of Australia helped to influence the decision of the British government to abandon the project, but the official *History of Northern Ireland in the Second World War* thinks that Nationalist demonstrations in Ulster during the critical week-end of 25 May 'were not entirely ineffectual'.[7]

There can be little doubt that behind a pro-conscription front the Northern Ireland cabinet was divided on the issue. Some wanted conscription because they felt that as loyalists they had to take their full share of the United Kingdom's burdens. Others opposed it because it would be unpopular with the Unionist rank and file, or because they did not wish to see large numbers of young Nationalists trained in the use of arms.

Some of these attitudes were publicly aired in the debates on the formation of a Local Defence Force to meet the threat of invasion. Lord Craigavon wished the force to be under his control because 'there is a fifth column,' he said, 'and we require to go very carefully along the road of arming people in Northern Ireland'.[8]

It became obvious that there was a difference of opinion between the government and the army over the control and constitution of the Defence Force. A military body under the control of Stormont would be a breach of the Government of Ireland Act, and a non-military body would contravene the laws of war. After further consultation Lord Craigavon announced that the 3,000 members of the R.U.C. and the 12,000 B-Specials would be reattested and enrolled in the army as a combatant force.[9] A few days later he abandoned this position and stated that there would be no reattesting or other formality.[10]

The status of the force was not finally settled till 1942

7. Blake, *op. cit.*, 198.
8. *Belfast Newsletter*, 22 May 1940.
9. *Ibid.*, 29 May 1940.
10. *Ibid.*, 31 May 1940.

when Defence Regulations were issued asking all members of the Ulster Special Constabulary to sign an undertaking to obey the Army Council, become subject to military law and give continuous unpaid service. There was no rush to accept these terms and even after months of persuasion many refused to sign.[11]

Two members of the cabinet resigned in disgust at the government's handling of the Defence Force project and its attitude to conscription and recruiting. One was the Parliamentary Secretary to the Ministry of Home Affairs, Mr J. E. Warnock, K.C. After a debate on the Home Guard in May 1940, Mr Warnock said, 'I am no longer a member of the Government. I have heard speeches about Ulster pulling her weight but they have never carried conviction . . .'.[12] In September Mr Warnock took the unprecedented step for a Unionist of moving a vote of censure. 'No limpet', he declared, 'clings to a rock with the tenacity with which members of the Government have clung to their posts.' He called for a drastic reconstruction of the government, stating that the Prime Minister by maintaining his present cabinet 'until the hand of God removes him' was not serving the province.[13] Two months later Lord Craigavon was dead. He was succeeded by one of the old guard, Mr J. M. Andrews, who was unable or unwilling to prise off the limpets.

The division of services between London and Belfast, described in the Government of Ireland Act as 'reserved' and 'transferred', was found to be an obstacle to the efficient prosecution of the war. It became necessary to by-pass or override the powers of the Northern government and various devices were found to do this.

The control of food supplies and of travel into and out of Northern Ireland were normally matters for the Northern government but in war time they were held to be reserved

---

11. Blake, *op. cit.*, 184.
12. *Hansard* (N.I.) xxiii, 1272 (28 May 1940).
13. *Hansard* (N.I.) xxiii, 2162 (25 Sept. 1940).

c

services. An officer of the Northern Ireland Ministry of Commerce was appointed Divisional Food Officer under the British Ministry of Food. Similarly, the issue of travel permits was in the hands of an officer of the R.U.C. who acted under the authority of the British Home Office. Extensive use was also made of Defence Regulations which gave the British Home Secretary power to delegate his functions in Northern Ireland as he saw fit. By this means even existing laws of the parliament of Northern Ireland were modified by regulations promulgated in London, and the powers of British ministers, such as the Minister of Labour, were extended to an area where normally they had no jurisdiction.

Not only was the authority of the Northern parliament overridden but its members were precluded from discussing the policies thus enforced. In a considered ruling by the Speaker, given at Stormont in 1940, they were informed that as the final responsibility for defence rested with parliament at Westminster they could not criticize the policies underlying the Defence Regulations.[14] With such restriction on discussion it is not surprising that parliament met on only twenty-five days in 1941.

After the fall of France in 1940 the realities of war gradually came home to Northern Ireland. The black-out was intensified. Unlighted streets, hooded car-lamps and darkened windows made city dwellers conscious of the phases of the moon. Moonlit nights meant danger. On nights of cloud and storm one could sleep soundly with little fear of being awakened by the air-raid sirens' wail. One could lie repeating the verses of the old Irish scribe in like circumstances:

Is acher in gaíth innocht,
fu-fuasna fairrgae findfolt;
ní ágor réimm mora mind
dond laechraid lainn ó Lothlaind.

14. Blake, *op. cit.*, 19–26.

(Bitter and wild is the wind tonight,
tossing the tresses of the sea to white;
on such a night as this I feel at ease,
fierce Northmen only course the quiet seas.)[15]

The south-west approaches were now effectively closed by German submarines and aircraft based on the French Atlantic coast. Convoys were routed via the north-west and escort vessels and patrolling aircraft operated from bases in Northern Ireland. Repair and supply depots were developed and a flying-boat base was established on Lough Erne. The state of the Belfast Harbour Commissioners, which included the shipyard, the aircraft factory and the miles of docks and warehouses, was the nerve-centre of the war effort. But 'vital though this area was,' writes the official historian, 'equipment could not be spared for its defence'.

In June 1940 not a single searchlight or mobile anti-aircraft battery was available in Northern Ireland and the defence of Belfast was entrusted to seven heavy guns. No other town in Northern Ireland had any defences at all.[16] In March 1941 the Minister for Public Security, Mr J. C. MacDermott, asked urgently for more guns, searchlights and night-fighters, saying with tragic prescience, 'the period of the next moon from, say, the 7 to the 16 April may well bring our turn'.[17]

A preliminary raid on 7 April tested the defences and found them negligible. The raiders returned in force on the night of 15/16 April when, according to German sources, 180 planes dropped 203 metric tons of bombs. More than 700 people were killed and a vast amount of damage was done to business premises, churches and dwelling-houses. In a second major raid on 5 May more than 200 planes dropped 96,000 incendiary bombs as well as high explosives on the

15. Translation by Prof. James Carney. Quoted in 'Early lyric poetry', a Thomas Davis lecture by Prof. M. Dillon in *Early Irish Poetry* (ed. J. Carney), Cork 1965.
16. Blake, *op. cit.*, 168.
17. Quoted by Blake, *op. cit.*, 168.

centre of Belfast causing severe damage in the harbour area. Though the loss of life was much less than on the previous raid (150 people were killed) the war effort received a serious setback. It was six months before Harland and Wolff returned to full production. The prompt aid rushed to Belfast on both occasions by the fire brigades of Dublin, Dún Laoghaire, Drogheda and Dundalk did much to wipe out the mistakes of twenty years of political posturing.

The Civil Defence Service was completely swamped by the aftermath of the raids. About 100,000 people were temporarily homeless. All accommodation in neighbouring towns and villages was submerged by the tide of refugees from the city. There should have been a Nye Bevan in Stormont to rend the government for its complacent bungling. There was only Tommy Henderson, Independent Unionist M.P. for Shankill, who dropped his clown's mask to cry out:

> I broke down after the things I saw. I broke down when I saw lying dead men I had been reared beside. When I saw the whole district where I roamed in my bare feet razed to the ground . . . Will the Right Hon. Member come with me to the hills and to Divis mountain? Will he go to the barns and sheughs throughout Northern Ireland to see the people of Belfast, some of them lying on damp ground? Will he come to Hannahstown and the Falls Road? The Catholics and Protestants are going up there mixed and they are talking to one another. They are sleeping in the same sheugh, below the same tree or in the same barn. They all say the same thing, that the government is no good.[18]

Against the background of common danger and bereavement traditional attitudes lost their validity. The guerrilla war between the R.U.C. and the I.R.A. became a private vendetta. The killing of a policeman, the conviction of six

18. *Hansard* (N.I.) xxiv, 828 (13 May 1941).

men on a capital charge and the hanging of one, raised hardly a ripple on the surface of the city's life.

The English novelist, F. L. Green, used war-time Belfast as the background of his *Odd Man Out*. This story of an I.R.A. man on the run, made into a film by Carol Reed, was a notable contribution to the art of the cinema but it had little relation to the realities of Belfast life. Brian Moore used the Civil Defence Service and the air-raids as thematic material for his novel *The Emperor of Ice-cream,* a harrowing story based on the author's service as an A.R.P. warden in Belfast.

After the raids there was a sharp rise in the number of unemployed. In the shipyard, aircraft factory and engineering works the out-of-work total rose from 1,700 in April 1941 to 5,800 in May. The linen industry was also in difficulties. In the first year of the war linen exports to the United States had been encouraged, but the fall of France had cut off the supply of flax and the introduction of Lease-Lend obviated the need to earn dollars. Some mills closed down and others were on short time. Unemployment in the industry rose to near its pre-war peak.[19]

The government hastened to compound its own sins by damning those of the Belfast Corporation. The report of an inquiry into the administration of Whiteabbey Sanatorium, made public in June 1941, disclosed, in the words of the Prime Minister, 'examples of mal-administration and worse'.[20] It found that some members of the Corporation Tuberculosis Committee 'failed to safeguard the interests of the ratepayers and the honour of the Council'.[21] It censured the Medical Officer of Health and the City Treasurer. The Minister of Home Affairs dissolved the T.B. Committee and gave the Corporation a month in which to reform. When it refused to do so, Commissioners were appointed to take control of the Corporation's finances. As officers of the Unionist Associ-

19. Blake, *op. cit.,* 542–4.
20. *Belfast Newsletter,* 3 July 1941.
21. *Ibid.,* 7 August 1941.

ation in the Duncairn Ward were involved in the scandal, some M.P.s thought that the government was reluctant to go to the root of the trouble, that the quarrel with the Corporation was a sham and that the Commissioners lacked real power.[22]

This dispute with the Corporation, the dissatisfaction with the war effort, the aftermath of the air raids, the continuing high rate of unemployment, produced a crisis in the Unionist Party. It lost three seats in bye-elections, including Lord Craigavon's old seat in North Down. Mounting criticism forced the Prime Minister to resign. He was replaced by Sir Basil Brooke who promptly jettisoned all the old guard, most of whom had been in office for more than twenty years.

Brooke had joined the government in 1929 as Assistant Parliamentary Secretary to the Minister of Finance. Appointed Minister of Agriculture in 1933 he had launched the war drive for increased tillage with energy and resource. In 1941 Andrews appointed him Minister of Commerce and he made this a key post in the cabinet, retaining it even after he became Prime Minister in 1943. He was the person to whom the Secretary of State delegated multifarious powers under Defence Regulations. He reorganized the Civil Defence Service after the air raids of 1941 but its efficiency was never tested. He pursued Whitehall with demands for more munition, and other, war contracts but his success was limited by the reluctance of the British government to embark on major schemes in Northern Ireland. Only with the arrival of American troops in Northern Ireland did he find both the opportunity and the means to show what he could do.

The first contingent arrived in January 1942. The build-up of infantry divisions and Army Air Force Squadrons went on steadily until by the end of 1943 there were more than 120,000 United States troops in Northern Ireland. Barracks were built, air-fields laid down, supply depots fitted out. This

22. *Hansard* (N.I.) xxiv, 1446–7 (9 Sept. 1941).

massive building programme was regulated by Sir Basil
Brooke's Production Committee which controlled the supply
and distribution of all bricks, cement, stone, tar and bitumen
in Northern Ireland. The output of broken stone from local
quarries went up from 400,000 tons a year to 400,000 tons
a month, and by August 1944 the number of unemployed had
dropped to 10,000, the minimum point on the curve.[23]

The presence of so many American servicemen, including large numbers of coloured troops, created problems for
the civil authorities. Young soldiers in country districts were
bored and got into mischief. They chafed against Ulster
sabbath restrictions. Their dollars attracted all the predators,
male and female, of the countryside. Confidential monthly
reports from the police to the cabinet showed that relations
with the civilian population were not always harmonious.[24]
The press was restrained in its reporting of incidents but
rumour magnified and distorted them. Many stories were in
circulation, some grave, some gay, some unprintable. A light-
hearted tale with an Ulster jag in it told of a meeting between two farmers over a drink on market-day. 'I see you
have the Americans near you, Jamie,' said one to the other.
'Aye,' replied Jamie. 'How do you get on with them?' asked
the first. 'Ach, they're all right. But I don't think much of
them white men they have wi' them.'

In the spring of 1944 the United States forces began to
leave Northern Ireland in preparation for the invasion of
France. The end of the war was in sight and the problems
of post-war reconstruction were clamouring for solution. The
air-raid damage to Belfast's slums had revealed the physical
damage done to the inhabitants by two decades of public
neglect. The condition of evacuees on arrival at reception
centres in the country shocked their hosts. Many children
were verminous; tuberculosis was rife among them. Social
workers discovered that maternity and child welfare services
were practically non-existent. A Select Committee appointed

23. Blake, *op. cit.*, 537.
24. *Ibid.*, 291–2.

to inquire into the health services found some of the evidence so alarming that a member stated 'We had to stop it [i.e. the inquiry] and ask the Minister for Home Affairs to take action'.[25] Sir Dawson Bates, the Minister responsible for public health as well as for the police, had built up Northern Ireland's huge and efficient police force at the expense of the health of the citizens. The Select Committee recommended the immediate creation of a Ministry of Health, and Sir Basil Brooke gave effect to this, nominating a former shipyard worker, Mr William Grant, as first Minister.

Another committee tackled the question of slum clearance and housing. It estimated that 100,000 new houses were required for immediate needs and a further 100,000 to eliminate overcrowding.[26] The Housing Acts of 1945 and 1946 provided subsidies from both state and local authorities for public and private builders. A Housing Trust, financed by the government but autonomous, was set up to build workers' houses in all areas of Northern Ireland. The sites developed by the Trust set high standards in building, layout and amenity. In spite of shortages of building materials and skilled labour the programme was pushed forward with vigour but the primary target of 100,000 houses was not reached till 1963.

The health services could not be remodelled until the British government had tabled its proposals for implementing the Beveridge Plan. Sir William Beveridge's *Report on Social Insurance and Allied Services,* published in 1943, advocated a state medical and health service and a comprehensive scheme of social insurance. The Northern Ireland Health Services Act (1948) was modelled on the English one. It abolished the old Poor Law Infirmaries and the dispensary system and set up a Board to provide medical and dental care for the entire population. It departed from the English model in establishing a separate Tuberculosis Authority, as tuberculosis was a special problem in Northern Ireland. The

25. Quoted by Lawrence, *op. cit.,* 139.
26. Lawrence, *op. cit.,* 152.

T.B. Authority was so successful that it was wound up in 1959 and its vestigial functions transferred to the Hospitals Authority.

The Board of Management of the Mater Hospital, the large and efficient Catholic teaching hospital in Belfast, refused to transfer its property to the Hospitals Authority. It received no share of the £12 million poured into the hospital service for capital expenditure by the Authority in the first ten years of its existence. It received no aid on current account either, although it helped the Authority to fulfil its statutory obligations.

The reform of Northern Ireland's education system effected by the Education Act (1947) also followed in general outline the English pattern. The public education system was divided into three stages, primary, secondary and further education. The school-leaving age was raised to fifteen and secondary education was provided for all up to that age.

The Northern government had tried since its inception to bring all primary schools into the state system and under the control of local authorities. Those managers of voluntary schools who held aloof were at first denied all grants for capital expenditure, but from 1930 onwards, grants of 50 per cent had been made available to them. In 1947 the majority of primary schools were still classified as voluntary but most of them were small and the number of pupils attending them was just under 50 per cent of the total. But of 77 secondary schools in existence at this date 67 were voluntary, among them the oldest, largest and most renowned schools of Ulster. They could neither be taken over nor ignored. Grants covering 65 per cent of capital expenditure were given to both primary and secondary voluntary schools and, in addition, the fees of children attending grammar schools were paid by the local authority provided they passed a qualifying examination.

The proposal to raise the voluntary school grant from 50 to 65 per cent caused a political crisis. Public attention was focused on the primary schools mostly under clerical management, and the grant was depicted as an endowment of the Roman Catholic Church. In 1949 the question arose again. Under the national insurance scheme, insurance cards for teachers had to be stamped by the employer. The Minister for Education, Lt. Col. Hall Thompson, held that as the state paid the teachers' salaries it was morally bound to pay the employers' contribution. Unionist backbenchers refused to allow this to be done for teachers in voluntary schools. The Grand Orange Lodge of Ireland discussed the matter and forced the resignation of the Minister.[27]

Northern Ireland would have found it impossible to finance these schemes for housing, health, education and social security had not Britain agreed to underwrite the cost.[28] In return Northern Ireland had to surrender much of the freedom given to her by the Government of Ireland Act. The Northern Ireland Budget and all supplementary estimates had to be submitted yearly to the Treasury for prior approval, and the Unemployment Insurance Fund, a transferred service under the 1920 Act, was virtually abolished when it was amalgamated with the British Fund as from July 1948.[29]

Many Unionists disliked the high taxation, financial restrictions and drift to socialism which were the price of social security. Some advocated dominion status for Northern Ireland in order to break the Treasury fetters on the economy. The leader of this movement was a Unionist M.P., Mr W. H. McCoy, K.C., and the ex-Prime Minister, Mr Terence O'Neill, has confessed that he was attracted to the movement when he first entered parliament.[30] But all discussion ended when the Unionist Party declared that the advocacy of dominion status was contrary to the principles of the party.

The Labour administration of Mr Attlee, which had so effectively buttressed Northern Ireland's economy, put the

27. *Belfast Newsletter,* 15 Dec. 1949.
28. See 'Health and Welfare Services in Northern Ireland', *Ulster Year Book* 1957–59.
29. See 'The Finances of Northern Ireland', *Ulster Year Book* 1950.
30. *Hansard* (N.I.) xlvi, 843 (15 March 1960).

coping-stone on its work by passing in 1949 the Ireland Act. This stated that 'in no event will Northern Ireland or any part thereof cease to be part of the United Kingdom without the consent of the Parliament of Northern Ireland'. The act was provoked by Mr Costello's petulant repeal of the External Relations Act. A curious side-reaction was the wiping out of all the Northern Ireland Labour Party's representation at Stormont. In the general election of 1949 all its candidates were defeated. The Unionist Party had stolen its thunder by copying the social legislation of Westminster, and Labour had antagonized its Catholic supporters by following the English lead and coming down firmly on the side of partition in an effort to capture the Protestant working-class vote.

The new leader of the Nationalist Party, Mr James McSparran, K.C., tried to unite all shades of national opinion under the broad label 'anti-partition'. He gave new vigour to parliamentary opposition in Stormont and he tried to win more active support from the South for an anti-partition campaign in Britain and throughout the world. It was hoped to bring the pressure of world opinion to bear on the British government which was ultimately responsible for the position of the minority in Northern Ireland. About 90 per cent of the revenue arising in Northern Ireland was due to taxes levied at Westminster. This money was then channelled back to Stormont by the British Treasury, due regard being given to the principle of parity. But there was no parity about its subsequent distribution. The case of the Mater Hospital has already been mentioned. The situation was similar in education. From 1923-46 £2 million was spent on state primary schools by the Minister of Education for new buildings and extensions but only £160,000 on voluntary schools. Yet there was approximately the same number of pupils in each type.

Catholics had built up a system of primary and secondary education which compared favourably with that provided by other bodies. They had established and maintained an efficient hospital in Belfast at a time when some of the hospitals of the local authorities were a menace to health. Now the

Catholic community was penalized because it refused to give up control of these. These were only some aspects of the discrimination which extended through the whole range of state and local government.

It is true, as Barritt and Carter point out in their survey, *The Northern Ireland Problem* (published 1962), that children's allowances, maternity grants, grammar school and university scholarships, benefit Catholics and Protestants alike, but it is not the whole truth. Social legislation greatly extended the area of state and local authority patronage, and in housing, health, transport and education the best jobs and the most lucrative contracts went to the government's supporters.

As Unionists became more wealthy their control of the machinery of local government became more secure, for not only was the local government franchise restricted to the wealthier citizens but limited companies were allowed a vote for every £10 of valuation up to a maximum of six votes. By this means and by manipulation of population movements through the control of housing or by adjustment of ward boundaries, areas such as Derry City or Omagh which have overall Nationalist majorities are firmly in Unionist hands. Since the Unionist Party equates Northern Ireland with the Party, such manipulation and discrimination are for it necessary conditions of existence.

Northern Ireland moved into the 1950s with few hesitations. Most of the social and economic ills which had beset it in the 1930s had apparently been cured. The benefits of the welfare state were eagerly accepted. The chains which bound it to the British economy hung loose as the ship of state floated free on the rising tide of taxation.

The Years of Readjustment, 1945-51

F. S. L. Lyons

'Mankind', said the poet, 'cannot bear too much reality.'
But he might have added that mankind cannot bear to be
without reality for too long. Or so at least the experience of
the Second World War seems to suggest. For although neutral
countries in war time have a hard enough reality of their own
to contend with, they are by definition excluded from the
even harsher reality experienced by the belligerents. For this
they have great cause to be thankful, but when the war is a
global one, the very isolation which serves them so well exacts
its own price. The price is that after the fighting is over the
process of adjustment to a strange new world is likely to be
exceptionally difficult for neutrals. And for the Irish, as for
others similarly situated, although an atmosphere of crisis was
never very far away between 1939 and 1945, the mere
physical, geographical and political facts of neutrality inevitably interposed a kind of screen, or glass, through which they
peered darkly at the storm outside. This screen was shattered
for many people by the easing of the censorship just at the
moment when the atrocities of the concentration camps were
being uncovered. And although Mr de Valera, in earlier
carrying his rigid doctrine of neutrality to the extreme of
expressing condolence on the death of Hitler, had been careful to observe that no judgement of any kind was involved,

67

the country as a whole had no difficulty in deciding where its sympathies lay. The war was hardly over before £3 million worth of food and clothing was sent to Western Europe and plans were laid to receive refugees from the stricken continent. But it very soon appeared that Ireland herself, though superficially undamaged by war, was in poor enough condition. She was short of houses, of fuel, of manufactures. Before 1945 was out the government had launched development programmes in building and rural electrification and these were followed in the next year by increased expenditure on agriculture. Unhappily, the summer of 1946 proved one of the wettest on record, and although Mr de Valera had previously appealed for an increase in wheat production, the yield was so bad that in 1947 bread rationing had to be introduced. The situation was aggravated by the fuel crisis in the early months of 1947, coinciding with one of the harshest winters of the century, with the result that industry and transport were almost paralysed and the public suffered severely. Meanwhile, in a natural reaction to war-time restrictions, people rushed to buy whatever was available. Inevitably, prices rose and imports increased. By contrast, wages lagged behind and so did exports. The now familiar bogey of the trade gap made its appearance and in the autumn of that miserable year a supplementary budget was necessary whereby taxes were raised to pay for higher food subsidies.

We can see now that all this was part of a larger web of circumstance in which most European countries were caught and, more specifically, that the recurrent pattern of Anglo-Irish economic relations in the post-war years was already taking shape, whereby England's difficulty was no longer Ireland's opportunity, but Ireland's difficulty also. At the time this was not so obvious and a mood of discontent began to spread through the country, no doubt intensified by the feeling that after sixteen years of Fianna Fáil, people were ready for a change. That autumn, government candidates were defeated at two bye-elections by representatives of a new party, Clann na Poblachta. One of the victors was the leader of the Clann, Mr Seán MacBride. As befitted the son of one of the executed men of 1916, he was dedicated to the idea of the Republic and the hard core of his following consisted of republicans (many of them I.R.A. men) who were prepared to try parliamentary methods provided they yielded rapid results. But the party also contained some of the rising younger men, notably Dr Noel Browne, who were more interested in social reform, and there can be little doubt that what most attracted the electorate to the Clann was its apparent combination of republican orthodoxy with social radicalism.

When the general election followed early in 1948 the Clann did not, as many expected, sweep the field, but the ten seats it did win gave it a pivotal position. Since Fianna Fáil lost ground it became clear that the other parties, if they could sink their manifold differences, had office within their grasp. After complicated negotiations the Inter-Party government emerged, containing representatives of Fine Gael, Clann na Poblachta, both Labour parties, the Farmers and the Independents. Their majority over Fianna Fáil was always precarious but the cohesive effects of power are very great and this 'tessellated pavement without cement'—to borrow Burke's phrase—was to last much longer than the pundits predicted. The coalition lived dangerously, certainly, and after three years of hectic life it went out in a blaze of controversy, but when its epitaph comes to be written two things will need to be remembered. One is that its survival for so long owed a lot to the new Taoiseach. The obvious choice, the Fine Gael leader General Mulcahy, was ruled out because of his part in the Civil War, and the job went to Mr Costello, a distinguished and widely respected lawyer. He proved an admirable chairman and even those who later differed with him on policy agree that his tact and patience did much to make cabinet meetings perhaps unexpectedly harmonious.

The other point that needs to be made unequivocally is that the Inter-Party government contained much talent and released a great deal of energy in projects of reform. But before these could take effect in domestic legislation the new government made a dramatic change in the relations of the state with the British Commonwealth. These were still governed by the External Relations Act passed by Mr de Valera before the war, under which, as he was still claiming in 1947, Ireland was a republic associated with the Commonwealth for matters of external policy. The Commonwealth issue had naturally figured in the election, but it seemed plain from the speeches of Fine Gael leaders that if returned to power they would not change the position, though it is also fair to say that some of them were unhappy about the ambiguities enshrined in the External Relations Act and would have liked to see those ambiguities cleared up. Clann na Poblachta, naturally, put the repeal of the act and the declaration of the Republic in the forefront of their programme. But another part of that programme, and indeed part of everyone's programme, was a renewed drive to end partition. What nobody made clear was how these aims could be reconciled in face of the passionate attachment of Northern Ireland to the Crown and the British connection.

This, however, did not prevent a massive propaganda campaign against partition being launched immediately after the Inter-Party government was formed. Indeed, the moment Ireland began to emerge on the world scene this was the theme of the message. At the Council of Europe, for example, from 1949 onwards the tirade against partition was repeated *ad nauseam* to a bored and largely uncomprehending Assembly. More seriously, when about the same time the Atlantic Alliance began to take shape, Ireland, though obviously deeply involved in western defence, refused to join so long as partition continued. But all this, as we can now see, was the merest beating of the air, achieving nothing. What *was* within the government's competence was to alter in a fundamental way the relationship with the Commonwealth. We still do not know enough about the balance of power within the cabinet to be able to say with certainty what pressures were exerted or by whom, but obviously Mr MacBride's

presence there must sooner or later have made the issue a
live one. Left to himself Mr Costello would probably not have
pushed it as far as it did in fact go, since his main interest at
that time was in economic reform. On the other hand, he was
dissatisfied with the External Relations Act, and he was also
deeply conscious of the way in which the idea of the Republic
had haunted and divided Irishmen ever since the Civil War.
If by settling this problem he could take the gun out of
politics, then he would feel justified in grasping the nettle.

As everyone knows he did grasp it before he had been
many months in office and in September 1948 announced in
Canada that the External Relations Act would be repealed.
Many myths have gathered round this celebrated Canadian
visit. The most notorious of these asserts that Mr Costello—
or Mrs Costello—was insulted by the Governor-General,
Field Marshal Alexander, and that in a rage Mr Costello
stormed off to a press conference and 'declared' the Republic
forthwith. Apart from the fact that this would have been
constitutionally impossible, the story is completely untrue. I
have recently consulted Mr Costello on this point and I am
grateful to him for giving me his authority for what I write
here.

First, it must be understood that *before* Mr Costello left for
Canada at all there had been a cabinet decision to repeal
the act. It is fair to say that one other minister whom I have
interviewed does not recall it, but this may be due to absence
from that meeting, or simply to the passage of years.
Certainly, although we shall probably not see the clinching
cabinet minute for many years, the evidence that such a
decision was taken is very strong. It rests not only on Mr
Costello's personal recollection, and on that of other ministers, but on Mr MacBride's subsequently published
testimony not only that the decision had been taken, but
also that at a meeting (held probably in August 1948) the
cabinet had considered and unanimously approved the text
of an important speech Mr Costello was to give in Canada
on 'Ireland in International Affairs'. Furthermore, Mr

MacBride himself had already in July stressed in the Dáil that in Anglo-Irish relations what mattered was the substance not the form. 'Outward forms', he added significantly, 'which are only reminders of a historically unhappy past can only act as irritants.' And early in August, again in the Dáil, the deputy prime minister, Mr Norton, had declared that 'it would do our national self-respect good at home and abroad if we were to proceed without delay to abolish the External Relations Act'. The timing of these important speeches has to be seen against the background of a parliamentary situation where there was a real possibility that a private member might at any time take the initiative and introduce a bill for repeal. This would presumably have received support from the opposition and would certainly have created great embarrassment for the Inter-Party government. The logic of this, as it presented itself to the cabinet, and as Mr Costello has since expressed it, was that 'if we were going to do it, we ought to do it at once'.

When Mr Costello arrived in Canada he was in the first instance a guest of the Canadian Bar Association at Montreal and made it clear to the press that while he was their guest he would make no comment of a political character. On 1 September he delivered to the Association the speech which the cabinet had already seen. It was a wide-ranging survey, and near the close he referred very plainly to 'the inaccuracies and infirmities' of certain provisions of the External Relations Act. This was in no sense a declaration of the Republic, but at least it indicated that Mr Costello took a fairly disenchanted view of the act. And the very next night he himself had evidence of at least one of these 'infirmities'. At the Bar Association dinner, after the toast of 'The King' had been given, the Canadian Minister for External Affairs said to him —'Doesn't that cover you?' 'I had to argue', says Mr Costello, 'that it did not because we were not real members of the Commonwealth.'

That was confusing enough, but confusion was soon worse confounded. On 4 September Mr Costello was the guest of the Canadian government at an official dinner in Ottawa given by Field-Marshal Alexander. This was the celebrated dinner round which legend has accumulated—with this much justification that during it Mr Costello had two unpleasant experiences. One was that at the Governor-General's table he was confronted with a replica of 'Roaring Meg', the famous gun used in the siege of Derry and ever since an almost sacred symbol to Ulster Unionists. This was not the most tasteful decoration with which to greet a Nationalist prime minister, but though it was irritating, it was not the stuff of which secessions are made. The other incident was more serious. It had been arranged by the Irish High Commissioner with the Canadian authorities that two toasts should be drunk—'The King' and 'The President of Ireland'. Yet, when the time came, only 'The King' was proposed. This was probably a simple error of protocol, though curiously enough Mr Costello had had a similar experience with Mr Attlee in Downing Street only a few months earlier. This incident, twice repeated, and involving in effect a denial of the existence of the Republic, certainly underlined what Mr Costello had already said about the 'inaccuracies and infirmities' of the External Relations Act. But, although he had come believing that both toasts would be proposed, he did not leave the dinner in a rage (any more than he had left the Montreal dinner) and he did not summon the press to declare the Republic.

What really precipitated his action in Canada was not these dinner-incidents but rather the appearance in next morning's *Sunday Independent* (5 September) of the headline —'External Relations Act to go'. It referred to Mr Costello's speech to the Canadian Bar Association, and also to those of Mr MacBride and Mr Norton I have already quoted, but whether the decision to run the story at that particular time was 'inspired' or not, must remain a matter of speculation. It should be said, however, that fourteen years later the *Sunday Independent* itself declared that its headline derived from 'an intelligent reading of Ministers' speeches'; perhaps this elegant formula should suffice. Mr Costello himself only learnt of the announcement by telephone late on Sunday afternoon. He was due to give a press conference on Tuesday, 7 September, and, as may be imagined, he spent the intervening thirty-six hours in anxious deliberation. However, he decided in the end to meet the inevitable question frankly and to say, as he did say, that it was his government's intention to repeal the act. This was the so-called 'declaration' of the Republic which caused such a stir in Ireland, even among ministers who, however aware of the original decision to repeal, could not, for obvious geographical reasons, have been able to help Mr Costello in the difficult problem of the timing of his announcement.

There followed the introduction in November of the necessary legislation, complete by the end of the year. In the debates Mr Costello stressed his intention both of ending bitterness within the country and of putting Anglo-Irish relations on a better, because a less ambiguous, basis. In reply to the argument that this step would make it even more difficult to end partition, he observed that refraining from it in the past had not evoked a single friendly gesture from Northern Ireland —why then continue to refrain from it in the future? This argument is not wholly convincing. Repeal might not have made a bad situation worse, but it surely meant that it would be harder in future to make that bad situation better. The legislation went through, however, with general support, for Fianna Fáil could not oppose it, though they might have been excused for feeling that the government had caught them bathing and stolen their clothes. Moreover, the clothes did not fit very well. What Mr de Valera had fought for all his life had been an all-Ireland, not a truncated, republic, and he could scarcely be expected to join in the celebration of the latter at the formal proclamation in April 1949. Whoever else's republic was born that Easter, it certainly was not Pearse's.

It might well be thought that such rapid and drastic action would have an adverse effect on relations with Britain. In the short run this may indeed have been so, but if there were ruffled feelings they seem to have been smoothed down very quickly. A step towards this was an important gathering at Chequers that autumn when Irish ministers met British ministers and representatives of the leading Commonwealth countries. At this meeting, it is said, the good offices of Canada and Australia were powerfully exerted. In the end, both Britain and the Republic safeguarded by legislation the rights of Irish citizens and British subjects in each other's countries. But the Ulster Unionists, as so often, had the last laugh, when they secured from the British parliament the Ireland Act of 1949 which, among other things, gave a solemn guarantee to Northern Ireland that it would never be detached from the United Kingdom without the consent of the Northern Ireland parliament. This provoked a storm of protest in the Republic and a great new wave of anti-partition propaganda, which was natural but in retrospect seems a little naïve. How could anyone ever have expected anything else?

With this issue out of the way it was possible to turn to constructive reforms at home. Some of these, admittedly, had been initiated by the previous administration, but there were certain new departures for which most of the credit must go to the Inter-Party government. Two, with which the dynamic Minister for Agriculture, Mr James Dillon, was particularly associated, were the great scheme of land reclamation providing state aid to bring 4 million acres into cultivation, and the 1948 trade agreement with Britain which secured favourable terms for Irish agricultural produce, especially by linking the price of store cattle and sheep to the guaranteed price received by British farmers for fat cattle and sheep. Others, which can only be briefly listed, were agricultural education on the parish level; co-operation with Northern Ireland in developing the Foyle fisheries; the unification of transport services under government control; the further development of the housing programme; and the virtual elimination of tuberculosis through the isolation of the disease in sanatoria where the new drug, streptomycin, could be effectively applied. Behind all this was Ireland's participation (which Fianna Fáil had set on foot) in the European Recovery Programme. Grants and loans from this source totalled nearly 150 million dollars by 1950 and without them the pace of expansion could not have been maintained.

Unfortunately, expansion brought with it a renewal of the disease with which Fianna Fáil had previously been grappling —galloping inflation. The coalition inherited from its predecessors an unhappy quarrel with the national school teachers (who had actually gone on strike in 1947) and to this was added an even more critical bank strike in 1950. These were indications of unrest among the white-collar workers and there is no doubt that in many families the rising cost of living, combined with the absence of social services comparable with those in Britain or Northern Ireland, was causing real hardship. The government was acutely conscious of this problem and tried to deal with both its aspects. Thus, in his very first budget Mr McGilligan cut expenditure in defence and other departments while increasing pensions for old people, widows and orphans. Nevertheless, inflationary pressure continued and early in 1951 the government had to freeze prices at the level obtaining in the previous December. But more positive methods were needed and at last, after long deliberation, an elaborate Social Welfare Bill was introduced in 1951. On 11 April it passed its second reading but on that very day a landmine exploded under the Inter-Party government. The crisis of what will always be known as the 'mother and child scheme' had come to a head.

As far back as 1947 Fianna Fáil had passed a Health Act intended to supply the basis of a national health service. It had had a difficult passage and parts of it had been challenged in the courts. However, when the Inter-Party government came to power the Minister for Health, Dr Browne, decided to bring in a scheme for maternal aid and child welfare which he hoped would apply without charge and without means test to such mothers (and their children up to the age of sixteen) as wished to use it. Although Dr Browne had become Minister the day he entered the Dáil, and was therefore totally inexperienced, his zeal for health reform had already brought great changes, among them the attack on tuberculosis previously noted. But his mother and child scheme soon ran into serious difficulties. Some came from the medical profession which in Ireland, as elsewhere, cast a cold eye on 'socialized medicine' and attacked both the absence of a means test and what seemed to them a tendency in the scheme towards excessive political control. This in itself, however, would scarcely have been decisive and in a straight fight the Minister would probably have beaten the doctors.

But of course it was not a straight fight. Dr Browne had to face far more ominous opposition when the Catholic hierarchy began to voice its objections to the scheme, as indeed it had previously voiced them to parts of the 1947 Act. In October 1950 these objections were conveyed to the Taoiseach. The hierarchy, it seemed, feared an invasion of family rights, the destruction of confidential relations between doctor and patient, the results which might flow from sex education by medical officers, and in general they felt that provision for the health of children was essentially a matter for the parents and that the state 'has the right to intervene only in a subsidiary capacity, to supplement, not to supplant'. Through a series of mishaps and misunderstandings Dr Browne seems genuinely to have believed that on paper and face to face with the bishops' representatives, he had met these objections, but when in March 1951 the matter was reopened it was clear that he had done nothing of the sort and that if no solution was found a serious situation would result. For a few weeks there was frantic correspondence and much coming and going, the evidence of which is all set out in *The Irish Times* for 12 April 1951 and in the Dáil debates for that same month. Dr Browne made an attempt later in March to reassure the hierarchy but failed to do so—they remained apprehensive both about the threat to faith and morals and about what they thought would be the damaging effects of the abolition of the means test.

By now it was clear that Dr Browne would not carry either his party or his colleagues with him. Mr Costello certainly was not prepared to cross the bishops in a matter involving faith and morals, and at meetings of Clann na Poblachta it appeared that some republicans, too, had a healthy respect for the hierarchy. On 10 and 11 April a sharp exchange of letters took place between Dr Browne and Mr MacBride, as a result of which, and at Mr MacBride's request, Dr Browne sent his resignation to Mr Costello on 11 April. The incident left an ugly taste behind it. It was easy for his opponents to blame Dr Browne for inexperience and fanaticism, but to the outsider it was the capitulation of the government to the bishops that was most disturbing. *The Irish Times,* for example, concluded that 'the Roman Catholic Church would seem to be the effective government of this country', and that a deadly blow had been struck at the anti-partition movement. The latter part of this statement was certainly correct, the former was exaggerated. The scheme did impinge on questions of faith and morals and that the Church should have intervened is neither surprising nor alarming. But what was and is alarming is the way in which the affair underlined the difficulty of drawing the boundary between morals and politics—the difficulty, in short, of reconciling parliamentary democracy with ecclesiastical authority. This is not impossible, but it needs eternal vigilance. And whether or not Dr Browne (as some suggested) was bent upon a clash, his sacrifice was not without reward. For such a crisis, revealed in all its intensity, was a warning both Church and state could not ignore. There has been no comparable collision since.

In the short term, however, the collision was fatal to the government. It had been losing prestige for some time, especially over the 'Battle of Baltinglass' where the Minister for Posts and Telegraphs had to withdraw his nomination to a postmastership in face of spirited, and sometimes richly comic, local resistance. More serious than this were the indications that Clann na Poblachta was breaking up. In

February 1951, Mr Noel Hartnett, an invaluable bridge between the republican zealots and the social reformers, resigned, declaring that the party had become obsessed with power and had abandoned 'any political or social philosophy'. Dr Browne's resignation was followed by others and in May Mr Costello decided to dissolve. After the general election it was not possible to rebuild the coalition and Fianna Fáil, with sixty-nine seats, was able to form a government. It was not much more firmly based than its predecessor, but it represented peace and quiet, which was what the electorate seemed to want. What they really wanted, one may suspect, was an economic leap forward into mid-century prosperity. They were not to get this for a few years yet, though by 1951 there were already premonitions of it. Meanwhile, the whole country seemed to be waiting, waiting—well, waiting, I suppose, for Mr Lemass.

Education and Language, 1938-51

DONAL McCARTNEY

Spontaneous enthusiasm for the language had marked the early years of the Gaelic revival. Since the decade before independence, however, preoccupation with political issues forced the ideal of an Irish cultural revolution into the background.

By the time independence had been achieved, stability restored and the prosaic business of running our own affairs had been tackled, much of the sort of enthusiasm that had been characteristic of the early years had evaporated. But the ideal remained. Besides, there was now for the first time control over the educational machinery which would be increasingly employed to effect the cultural revolution. All political parties agreed that the restoration of Irish must be a primary objective of the young state. The great cultural adventure was on, and the baby was handed over to the Department of Education.

Education and the language became inextricable threads in the fabric of Irish society. Debate on the one tended inevitably to raise the question of the other. A presidential address to the Annual Congress of Secondary Teachers in 1947 complained that scarcely any minister of state or public figure ever mentioned education other than in connection with the revival of the Irish language.[1]

1. See *School and College Year Book* 1948–9, 8.

Under the Free State government the policy had been initiated of using the schools as the main weapon in the fight for the restoration of the language.

That policy was accepted also by Fianna Fáil, continuously in office from 1932 to 1948. Mr Derrig, who was Minister for Education during most of this period, often stated that in the question of Irish in the schools he was merely continuing the policy of Mr Cosgrave's regime. The only difference between Fianna Fáil's policy on the language and that of the previous government was one of degree: under Fianna Fáil the drive for Irish was intensified.

The national objective was the restoration of Irish. A major difficulty arose, however, from the fact that the restoration of the language meant different things to different people.

First of all there were those who wished to see Irish as the sole vernacular of the country and who felt that Irish could not replace English quickly enough. They took the line that logically we could not have Irish and English on the same level—the people would speak Irish or English but not both. It was a war to the death for the Irishman's tongue. Bilingualism was a stage but not the objective. In the Dáil this point of view was represented by Fianna Fáil deputies Alderman Cormac Breathnach and Donnchadh Ó Briain. Tomás Ó Deirg, when, for instance, he claimed in 1943 that we could not save Irish 'without waging a most intense war against English, and against human nature itself for the life of the language', clearly belonged to this camp.[2]

The members of this group did not always feel so sure about Mr de Valera. His Constitution of 1937 had described English as the second official language of the state. And when for a short period in 1940 he was Minister for Education as well as Taoiseach, he hinted that had he been in office in the 1920s he would have been very slow to introduce the teaching

2. This was the official translation of the Minister's speech delivered in Irish. It was quoted and attacked by Professor O'Sullivan, former Minister, and by General Mulcahy, future Minister, see *Dáil Éireann, Parliamentary Debates,* xc, 105, 176, 12, 13 May 1943.

of other subjects through Irish until children had been given a good foundation in the language. He also held that a certain amount of latitude should be given to the teachers in the use of English as a medium of instruction, and said that if convinced of the necessity he would be prepared to consider reforms with regard to teaching through Irish.[3] This kind of statement made Donnchadh Ó Briain in the Dáil a trifle uneasy about Mr de Valera's position, and brought forth a strong protest in the pages of *The Leader*.[4] They were views which seemed to place Mr de Valera in the camp of those who wished to see Ireland bilingual rather than merely Gaelic.

And the Taoiseach did differ from more extreme revivalists, especially on the question of timing. According to Mr de Valera's view the schools were trying to get the children fluent in two languages. Then within a reasonable time he wanted the people to be able to speak Irish as naturally as they now spoke English. Ultimately he wanted Irish to be the universal language in this country.[5]

There was a third group among revivalists, and the people who belonged to this group understood the restoration of Irish to mean not the replacement of English, or any lowering of our standards in that language but merely the wider use of Irish in the life of the country. Mr Lemass was sometimes popularly taken to belong to this group.

These different and for the most part non-articulated interpretations of the national objective did not make the task of revival any easier and sometimes in practice led to confusion and conflict.

3. *Dáil Éireann, Parliamentary Debates*, lxxx, 1569–70, 1637, 6 June 1940.

4. See *The Leader*, 15 June 1940, 438. This editorial comment (believed to have been written by Mr Earnan de Blaghd) said that Mr de Valera had 'definitely let down the Irish language', that his policy regarding it showed him to be 'a kind of waking Rip Van Winkle who went to sleep in 1916', that nearly all his decisions were 'unhelpful if not positively harmful' and that it was feared that before he was done with it 'the language would not only be let down but actually betrayed'. Shortly afterwards when Mr Derrig returned to his post he was welcomed back by *The Leader* which rejoiced that Mr de Valera had gone from the Department of Education (*The Leader*, 29 June 1940, 489).

5. *Dáil Éireann, Parliamentary Debates*, lxxx, 1628, 6 June 1940.

The Department of Education, however, never had any doubts about what the national objective entailed for the schools. The schools, as Mr Derrig often re-affirmed, were to be regarded as the main, and perhaps in many cases the sole, instrument of restoring Irish. He said that he fully appreciated that in no other country in the world had such a task been laid on the schools. Our teachers had not alone to teach the children to speak their national language, a huge task in itself, but, in the course of their work, said Mr Derrig, they had to contend with the indifference of the general public as well as with the open and veiled hostility of certain sections.[6] The work which the Department had taken on was to ensure that the pupil would emerge from the primary school at fourteen years of age capable of using Irish as his vernacular and desirous of doing so.

The first step was to produce Irish-speaking teachers. The task was formidable enough, but the progress was impressive. In 1922 only 1,107 teachers in the primary schools were qualified to teach through Irish.[7] Around 1932 a noticeable expansion in the numbers began as a result of the intake into the profession of teachers who had been educated in the residential Preparatory Colleges. By 1943 there were some 9,000 (representing two thirds of the total number of teachers) qualified to conduct education through Irish. It was felt to be only a matter of time until all teachers were well-equipped to achieve the goal of a Gaelicized educational system at primary level.

The pupils and the schools soon responded to the new situation. In 1931 228 schools were listed as teaching all subjects through Irish. Then with the increase in the number of teachers qualified with the Bilingual Certificate the figures for the all-Irish primary schools rose impressively during the early years of the Fianna Fáil government until by 1939 the figure was 704 schools. That is, nearly 14 per cent of the primary

6. *Dáil Éireann, Parliamentary Debates,* lxxiv, 2425-6, 23 March 1939.
7. This figure and the other statistics in this chapter are based upon the official Reports of the Department of Education for the years 1938–51.

schools provided an all-Irish education, while another 46 per cent were teaching partly through Irish.

The figure of 704 schools in 1939 teaching entirely through Irish was numerically the high-water mark. Right through the war and its aftermath the number of all-Irish primary schools fell drastically. In 1944 there were a hundred less than in 1939. In 1951 they numbered only 523. And the decline continued.

What had gone wrong with the plan for the Gaelicizing of the primary system? One thing is clear: it cannot be explained merely by any decrease in the number of schools in the Gaeltacht.[8] For in 1939, 43 per cent of the all-Irish schools were outside the Gaeltacht but in 1951 this had dropped to 38 per cent. This would point to the conclusion that it was not the failure to save the Gaeltacht so much as failure to convert the Galltacht which explains these diminishing returns.

From the information supplied by the inspectors, the Department was mildly jubilant in 1939 about the progress of the Gaelicizing policy. In the official *Report* for that year it was stated that if the language was dependent on the schools alone then it could be claimed that it was out of danger. In the following year, however, criticisms of the teachers for not speaking more Irish among themselves and with their pupils or suggestions as to how they might speed up the Gaelicizing policy in the schools became a regular feature of the annual *Reports* of the Department. Nevertheless these official *Reports* always stressed that there was a continuous and gradual progress towards the goal that had been set. But in 1944 and again in 1948 the Department admitted that it was not possible to say that the aim to make Irish-speakers out of children leaving the schools at 14 years of age had yet been reached in the majority of schools.

One important thing which militated strongly against the

8. The *Gaeltacht* is the name for those parts of Ireland where Irish is mainly spoken. The *Galltacht* is the name for the rest of Ireland where English is mainly spoken.

achievement of further progress was the fact that relations between the teachers' organization (the I.N.T.O.) and the Department of Education were far from cordial during much of this period. Three major areas of disagreement emerged during these years—first, the whole question of Irish in the schools, second, the introduction of the compulsory Primary Certificate in 1943, and third, a long drawn out salary dispute. As often happens in such circumstances, these disputes were not isolated and treated separately from each other : on the contrary each area of disagreement between the I.N.T.O. and the Minister added bitterness to the other. Dissatisfaction among the teachers inevitably hampered the language drive in the schools.

Ideologically the I.N.T.O. and the Department of Education were in the same camp—they were both committed to the language revival. But in 1941 the I.N.T.O. issued its *Report* on Irish in the schools.[9] This *Report* pointed to the conclusion that the progress made was disappointing and that the damage done was considerable. It claimed that more than half of the teachers replying to a questionnaire thought that they were being coerced in some way or other into doing what they felt they were unable to do. And reform of the methods used in the schools was called for.

Before the publication of the I.N.T.O. *Report,* uneasy feelings—some of them vague enough—had been expressed from time to time about the language policy of the Department of Education. In the Dáil the irrepressible James Dillon was the most constant and articulate critic of the policy of teaching through Irish. He claimed that the method was destroying disinterested enthusiasm for the language; that it created antipathy to Irish among children and parents; and that it was doing serious damage by lowering the general educational standard.

Individual critics may not have been taken seriously. But

9. The full title is *Report of the Committee of Inquiry into the Use of Irish as a Teaching Medium to Children whose Home Language is English.*

the *Report* of the teachers' organization had the effect of making many feel doubtful about the methods in use. It was John Marcus O'Sullivan who, as Minister for Education, had sponsored the language policy in the 'twenties. Now after the publication of the I.N.T.O. *Report*, Professor O'Sullivan, while still believing the general policy pursued to be the right one, said that it seemed to him that the I.N.T.O. had made an unanswerable case for an investigation. In any case, he argued, it would not be wise for his successor in office to flout the opinion of those on whose co-operation in the schools he depended.[10]

Mr Derrig was not to be moved. He argued that aspects of the I.N.T.O. *Report* were not above criticism, and that only when all teachers were qualified would it be fair to take stock of the position. Meanwhile his appeal to the teachers to apply some of the spirit of the early Gaelic League workers fell upon hardening hearts and deaf ears.

For apart altogether from the language, other circumstances contributed to make these years difficult and unpleasant ones for the teachers. A continuous decline in the school-going population resulted in the closure, the amalgamation and the non-replacement of schools. In 1951, and despite the erection of many big and bright schools especially in the newly developed areas of the cities, there were 287 primary schools fewer than there had been 13 years earlier. The falling off in the number of pupils on the rolls, and in the number of schools, threatened many teachers with the loss of their positions, and many others with the loss of allowances and promotion prospects. To deal with the situation the Department closed temporarily avenues of recruitment for national teachers. Morale among the teachers was extremely low. By contrast prospects were much brighter in the secondary and vocational schools where the number of buildings and of pupils continued to expand.

National teachers were also very dissatisfied with their salary

10. *Dáil Éireann, Parliamentary Debates*, xc, 105–7, 12 May 1943.

position. An invidious rating system existed whereby the Department's inspectors graded teachers as 'highly efficient', 'efficient' or 'non-efficient'. About one in every three teachers was invariably rated as 'highly efficient' and was entitled to a higher salary than his colleagues. The system was open to many abuses in teaching practice, it led to discontent among the teachers and it poisoned relations between the inspectors and the inspected. The Department's officials were going round more like spies than inspectors, said Mr Jack Lynch in his maiden speech on education in the Dáil in May 1948.[11]

Protracted salary negotiations between the teachers and the Minister ended when a final offer by the Minister was submitted to a ballot of all members of the I.N.T.O. in the Twenty-six Counties and rejected by a majority. This was followed by the controversial strike of teachers in the Dublin schools in 1946 which lasted from March to October. An offer to mediate by the Catholic archbishop of Dublin was rejected by a government which remained adamant and eventually the teachers returned at the request of the archbishop.

The strike of the teachers had deep repercussions. In such circumstances the position of Irish in the schools was certainly not enhanced. The bitterness of the strike together with the fact that the language was bound up with the teachers' efficiency rating and advancement prospects created a very undesirable atmosphere. And as a result the language lost considerable ground and prestige in the schools during the 1940s. Meanwhile the I.N.T.O. had emerged as one of the most militant groups in the country. And when Fianna Fáil fell from office in 1948 the trouble with the teachers was one of the causes of the loss of votes. For a feature of the emergence of Clann na Poblachta as a force in Irish politics in these years was the number of teachers who were associated with it.

11. *Dáil Éireann, Parliamentary Debates,* cx, 1153, 4 May 1948.
D

At a time when the vast majority of our children (about 9 in 10) received no formal education beyond the age of 14 the comparative failure of the language policy in the primary schools meant a corresponding failure elsewhere in the educational system and indeed throughout society generally. As in the case of the primary schools, the progress of the language at post-primary level was more impressive-looking on paper than in reality.

In the sphere of secondary education, the Department behaved somewhat like a benevolent headmaster distributing prizes so as to encourage the more extensive use of Irish. A special capitation grant was paid out to schools which taught subjects through Irish; a special increment was paid to teachers who used Irish as the medium of instruction, and a bonus in examination marks was awarded to students who answered through Irish. The scheme introduced in 1933-4 whereby a grant of £2 was paid for every child of primary school-age who lived in the Gaeltacht or Breac-Gaeltacht and whose normal home language was Irish had some success in slowing down the Anglicizing of peripheral Gaeltacht areas. This scheme was extended in 1945 to include all school-going children up to 16 years of age and the grant was increased to £5. The number of children who benefited by the grant remained fairly constant around 10,000. Inducements such as these had some of the desired effects and the number of secondary schools teaching through Irish increased steadily up to the early 1940s. In 1941 and 1942 64 per cent of all pupils in the secondary schools were being instructed through Irish or partly through Irish. From then on the Department fought a losing battle. Despite an increase introduced in 1944-5 in the special capitation grants for schools teaching through Irish, and despite an extra grant from 1946 for schools whose pupils showed proficiency in oral Irish, the number of pupils receiving instruction through Irish dropped steadily to 54 per cent in 1951.

Among the reasons for the decline was the difficulty of studying subjects in a language in which the students were not really proficient, and the absence of suitable textbooks in Irish.

Only an optimist could claim that the comparatively large numbers who completed a course of secondary education through Irish were in fact capable of using it as the vernacular and willing to do so. The fact that a student held a Leaving Certificate with honours in Irish and that he had answered other subjects through Irish was no guarantee whatever that he was capable of carrying on a conversation fluently in the language. For this anomaly of our educational set-up the examination system was largely to blame.

The national aim was to revive Irish as a *spoken* language, and in this our schools were expected to play the major role. Yet our educational system was so dominated by the written examination that spoken Irish was neglected. In 1943 the regulations governing the Primary Certificate were altered so as to require that all sixth standard pupils in the future would be presented for examination. A later Minister for Education, Mr O'Malley, has been reported as saying in the Senate that he had no hesitation in publicly pronouncing his utter disgust for the Primary Certificate form of examination.[12] But when it was introduced in 1943 it was strongly defended by Mr de Valera and Mr Derrig and as strongly condemned by the I.N.T.O. and it never received the full co-operation of the teachers. Where the Primary Certificate was taken seriously by the teachers, it encouraged a concentration on the techniques of written examination at the expense of the spoken word.

Concentration on the written examination was even more pronounced for the Intermediate and Leaving Certificates. Up to 1939 the subject matter to be studied in the secondary schools was not prescribed. Within certain limits the choice of what was to be studied was left to the individual teacher. The method had a great deal in its favour. It was felt, however, that it placed too much of a burden on both

12. *The Irish Times,* 6 May 1967, 6.

teachers and pupils, and an examination programme which prescribed in detail the matter for study was introduced instead.

With this new programme the memorizing of a large number of set poems in Irish and in English and of so-called 'appreciations' of set texts became an evil feature of our educational system. The ability to memorize and to regurgitate was exalted at the expense of the higher faculties of the intellect. Our secondary schools with their academically-biased curriculum and their preoccupation with written-examination results turned out ready-made seminarians, civil servants and clerks of all descriptions. Their success in turning out Irish-speaking enthusiasts was not so notable.

From the point of view of the Irish enthusiast the position of Irish in university education was also unsatisfactory. Galway, the smallest of the constituent colleges of the National University, provided degree courses through Irish in Arts, in Commerce and in certain Science subjects. Appointment to lecturing positions in Cork normally required the candidate to show fluency in Irish although teaching through Irish was not afterwards expected. In U.C.D. the students had to pass a test in oral Irish but this proved to be so unsatisfactory that it has since been abolished. The pressure which Irish enthusiasts tried to exert in higher education did not go unchallenged. A very significant battle between the Irish enthusiasts and their opponents occurred in 1943 over the appointment to a Chair of Education. The man who was eventually successful got strong support in U.C.D. but his candidature had been strongly contested on the grounds of his lack of Irish. The defeat of the Irish enthusiasts on this particular issue showed that many in high positions in university circles did not share the view that Irish was a necessary qualification for a professor of education. It was an important and critical defeat for Irish enthusiasts for had they been successful on that occasion it would have been more difficult in the universities to resist further pressures. In the Dáil a deputy claimed that no greater insult could have been offered to the language, and by an institution which might have been expected to be the spearhead of national ideals. The people, he added, had not been given much inspiration from the top by such an incident.[13] This defeat of the enthusiasts corresponded with the general slowing down in the progress of the Gaelicizing policy and with a mounting opposition to that policy throughout the educational system.

The war years, by distracting attention from education and by disturbing the economic life of the country, had hindered educational development. It was a time when educational research, discussion and ideas were both scarce and ineffective. So far as education was concerned this period was not our finest hour. After the war we were slower to tackle the problems of educational reform than countries which had suffered more. For these countries emerged with the determination to build from the bottom and in this re-building, education was considered a priority. We, who had less to re-build, tended to carry on longer in the pre-war educational groove. Britain, on the other hand, while still at war had introduced the famous Education Act of 1944 which among other things extended free secondary education to all who desired it. A couple of years later Northern Ireland followed with a scheme based on that of Britain.

Partly as a result of these developments in the neighbouring states, dissatisfaction with the condition of education in this country became more widespread. And because the drive for Irish was associated with a system of education that was now coming in for much criticism, the emphasis on Irish in the schools was often unfairly blamed for the weaknesses in the educational system. Mr Derrig's admission, however, that there would have to be sacrifices in other areas and some educational waste for the sake of the language gave some point to the charge.[14]

13. *Dáil Éireann, Parliamentary Debates*, xc, 186, 13 May 1943.
14. *School and College Year Book* 1941–2, 8.

Discontent, however vague, with our educational system was one of the factors which contributed to the change of government in 1948. So widespread had this discontent become that some people feared that the Inter-Party government might attempt radical changes with regard to Irish in the schools. Thus several speakers on the Fianna Fáil benches (including two later Taoiseachs, Mr Lemass and Mr Lynch) expressed relief that General Mulcahy, a dedicated revivalist, had been given charge of education.[15] Mulcahy bowed to some of the winds of criticism that were blowing and accepted some of the proposals for reform that had been aired in recent years. The system of rating teachers was abolished in 1949. A Council of Education was established in 1950 and given its first task of advising the Minister on the function of the primary school and on the curriculum to be pursued. And it was proposed to enquire into the position of Irish.

To sum up : it was possible, on paper at least, to show progress in the drive for the Gaelicizing of our educational system up to the years 1939-42. From the early 1940s the machine began to creak and the progress was halted. Saturation point seemed to have been reached. The early enthusiasm of the teachers and of the schools had been spent. General apathy and indifference outside the schools had not been overcome. Criticism of the methods employed grew and became more respectable.

Those responsible for policy-making and administration had not faced the issue of whether the sights had been aimed too high and whether a policy of more limited objectives for each generation might not have been more just and have had more success than the all-out offensive to turn a generation of school-children into Irish-speakers. In the early days of the cultural revolution young men and women had shown the kind of enthusiasm and energy that was needed if the revival was to succeed. But in the first 30 years of our independence we had in practice thrown the tremendous responsibility for

15. *Dáil Éireann, Parliamentary Debates*, cx, 57, 1151, 18 Feb., 4 May 1948.

the language restoration on to the shoulders of children of 14 years and younger. And this was done without any sufficiently imaginative appeal to win over their good-will and enthusiasm. It is at least arguable that we had concentrated our efforts on the wrong age-group.

An excessive touchiness on the part of some enthusiasts interpreted every criticism of the revival methods as an attack on the language. And the anxiety to advance too rapidly did serious damage to the cause. Revival efforts had been guided more by principle than by method. The need to qualify in Irish at examinations and for positions of employment seemed to some to be an unpleasant and unnecessary addition to the hardships of life. And where these tests in Irish were no more than a formality they encouraged hypocrisy in some people and cynicism in others.

What the direction of the language revival demanded was an attitude of mind that was enthusiastic yet prudent, imaginative, constantly fresh, original and adaptable. Given such an attitude the revival would still have been far from easy. However, all it got in these years was the Department of Education, whose function was primarily non-creative, and which was understaffed and preoccupied with the everyday business of administration.

In these circumstances the Department's ambitions to Gaelicize all the schools and turn out Irish speakers were not realized. Or, put another way, the Department of Education had failed the Irish test which had been set by the state.

Industry and Labour

DONAL NEVIN

During the nineteen thirties, the protectionist policy pursued by the Fianna Fáil government led to the establishment of many new industries. The factories that were set up behind the shelter of high tariff walls were for the most part small-scale concerns, dispersed widely throughout the country and concentrating mainly on the production of light consumer goods for the home market. Much-needed employment was provided in cities and towns in these factories though frequently high costs of production and a low level of efficiency meant higher prices for consumers.

Thus by the outbreak of war in 1939 there was in existence a small industrial sector giving employment to one person in six of the working population. This comparatively weak industrial arm was to play a vital part in the maintenance of supplies during the war years. During these years severe difficulties were experienced by industry on account of the cessation of imports of some essential raw materials, a scarcity of replacement parts for machinery, a shortage of new equipment, low-quality fuel. By minor miracles of ingenuity and improvisation the wheels of industry were kept turning. Nevertheless some factories were to close down completely while many maintained a precarious existence.

By 1944 the output of industry had fallen to about three

94

quarters of the pre-war level.[1] Employment in industry fell less sharply though some industries, notably building, suffered severely. Many thousands of industrial workers experienced frequent spells of unemployment and a great many were on more or less continuous short-time.

The conditions of the time imposed severe hardship on workers and widespread distress prevailed. While the cost of living soared, wages were rigidly controlled, resulting in a sharp fall in workers' living standards. Unemployment grew notwithstanding a high level of emigration—the Registers of Population taken in 1941 and 1943 revealed that net emigration in this two-year period totalled 85,000.[2] With the severe cutback in the building of new houses, housing conditions deteriorated. Social welfare benefits—like wages—failed to keep pace with the rising cost of living, so that poverty was widespread and for a great many was indeed acute.

The war years were to present the Labour movement with a challenge and an opportunity. The social unrest and industrial discontent were such that it seemed Labour must at last win the support of increasing numbers of urban workers so that at the end of the war it would be poised for a great advance both industrially and politically. The end of the war, on the contrary, was to find the Labour movement divided and in disarray.

The expansion in industrial employment in the 'thirties had meant a rising trade union membership and in 1939 it amounted to about 150,000 for the Twenty-Six Counties area.[3] Membership of the unions was predominantly industrial and as yet only limited sections of white-collar and professional employees were organized. The structure of the movement, the product of historical circumstances rather than design, had remained largely unaltered from the

1. *Statistical Abstract,* 1947–1948, table 88.
2. *Statistical Abstract,* 1946, table 6.
3. David O'Mahony, *Industrial Relations in Ireland: The Background,* Economic Research Institute, Dublin 1964, 9.

beginning of the century, a mixture of craft, industrial and general unions with a weak central authority. There were among the leaders of the trade union movement men of great ability, experienced organizers, effective negotiators, but there was much personal animosity and distrust. There was, too, a deep division of opinion as to the future organizational structure of the movement. Ideologically the unions sub-scribed—nominally at least—to the teachings of James Connolly but the earlier revolutionary ardour had evaporated, the vision of a new society all but fled. Above all, the old antagonism between William O'Brien, the general secretary of the Irish Transport and General Workers' Union and Jim Larkin, the general secretary of the Workers' Union of Ireland, still smouldered, soon to blaze fiercely and to split the Labour movement into two camps.

In 1941 two events of great significance for the trade unions occurred. The first of them, the introduction of the Wages Standstill Order, galvanized the movement into united action. The second, the introduction by Mr Seán MacEntee, the then Minister for Industry and Commerce, of the Trade Union Bill, was indirectly to widen the fissures within the trade union movement.

The Wages Standstill Order—the Emergency Powers Order No. 83—came into operation in May 1941. It effectively prohibited any increases in wages and prevented unions from striking for higher wages by removing the legal protection of the Trade Disputes Act from such strikes. This unprecedented measure aroused intense opposition from all the trade unions. It was only from April 1942 that workers were permitted to obtain any increases in wages and even these were to be related to *future* increases in the cost of living.

The opposition by the trade unions to the government's wages policy was unavailing. Trade unionists contrasted the iron-control maintained over wages with the opportunities for profiteering and black market dealings that the shortages of supplies provided. The Irish Trade Union Congress complained that 'open profiteering and the black market in rationed and unrationed commodities had reached the dimensions of a national scandal'.[4] The unrest and agitation that Order No. 83 provoked was, however, contained.

Up to September 1946 when the emergency control of wages was revoked—five and a half years after its introduction—the maximum permissible wage increase payable under the various bonus orders was only 16 shillings per week.[5] The effect of the Wages Standstill Order in depressing workers' living standards is clearly evident in the comparison between the increase in wages and the increase in prices over the war period. Between 1939 and 1946 the cost of living index, as it was called, rose by about two thirds but the average weekly earnings of industrial workers rose by only one third.[6]

There was united trade union opposition to the Wages Standstill Order, which William O'Brien was to describe as 'provocative, ill-advised and a grave blunder on the part of the Government'.[7] Not so united, however, was the opposition to the same government's Trade Union Bill. The bill, which had a two-fold purpose, did give rise to a storm of protest but the protest was decidedly muted in some quarters. In the first place this bill provided that only licensed trade unions could carry on negotiations for fixing wages or other conditions of employment, and before being licensed, trade unions had to deposit substantial sums of money with the High Court. The second main feature of the bill—and a more controversial one—was the establishment of a Trade Union Tribunal whose members would be appointed by the Minister. This tribunal could determine that one union alone should be entitled to organize a particular class of workers

4. *Forty-eighth Annual Report of the Irish Trade Union Congress*, 1942, 33.

5. For the detailed provisions relating to the control of wages during the war see *Some Statistics of Wages and Hours of Work in* 1946, Department of Industry and Commerce, Dublin 1948, 6–9.

6. *Statistical Abstract*, 1947–1948, tables 241 and 258.

7. *Forty-seventh Annual Report of the Irish Trade Union Congress*, 1941, 76.

where the union could show that it organized a majority of the workers in that particular class.

The ostensible purpose of this Part III of the bill was the rationalization of the trade union movement. The proposal touched a trade union sore spot in that there had been much talk but little progress made towards re-organizing the movement along more rational lines. It touched a sorer spot in that it proposed that only an Irish-based union could be given sole negotiating rights by the tribunal. (In fact the Supreme Court held in 1946 that this part of the Trade Union Act was invalid as it was in its main principles repugnant to the Constitution.)

This part of the bill, however, was not questioned by the Irish Transport and General Workers' Union. William O'Brien, its general secretary, in his address as president of the Irish T.U.C. in 1941, spoke of the bill in a guarded way. Having noted that for years the trade union movement had been in urgent need of reorganization, he recalled that in 1936 they had been warned by the government that unless they put their own house in order the government would be forced to do so. In that year, the Congress had set up a representative commission to consider ways and means of reorganizing the movement but, in Mr O'Brien's words, 'the only result was complete and absolute failure and as a consequence of this failure we now have governmental interference in our movement in a manner that is quite naturally resented but for which we ourselves are largely responsible'. He added—and the point was not lost on the delegates to the Congress—that 'no matter what the proposals in the measure were, there would be an outcry from the superfluous unions which we all want to see eliminated—or, to use an expression in fashion in some quarters, "liquidated" '.[8]

In Dublin a Council of Action was formed by the Dublin Trades Union Council to oppose the Trade Union Bill. The I.T.G.W.U., however, which had earlier withdrawn from the

8. *Ibid.*, 76–7.

Dublin Trades Union Council when that body accepted Larkin's union, the Workers' Union of Ireland, into membership, remained aloof from the campaign. Larkin himself took a leading part in it and it culminated in a huge demonstration in College Green where in the course of a stirring speech Larkin, in a typical gesture, held aloft a copy of the Trade Union Bill and set it alight.

Portents of the approaching split were evident at the annual conference of the Irish T.U.C. in 1941. None of the 39 delegates from the Irish Transport and General Workers' Union spoke during the lengthy debate on the Trade Union Bill and Larkin was not contradicted when he told the delegates of a deputation to the Taoiseach and the Minister for Industry and Commerce at which Mr MacEntee had stated that the bill had not come of his initiative and that what he was doing was with the knowledge and approval of some trade union officials whom he declined to name.[9] Significantly the delegates to the Congress insisted on referring back the section of the report which dealt with the Trade Union Bill on the grounds that not enough had been done by the Congress to oppose it.[10]

This 1941 Congress was the first occasion since 1914 that Larkin had spoken at the Irish T.U.C. and, ominously, he had clashed sharply with the president, William O'Brien. Larkin spoke as a delegate from the Dublin Trades Union Council since his union's application for affiliation to the Congress had consistently been refused because, to quote the Congress report, 'its record as a cause of disruptive action against the Trade Union Movement and promoter of libels against officers of affiliated unions and of Congress itself would make its admission a disintegrating instead of a harmonizing element within Congress'.[11] In the dissension that was soon to split the Labour movement, the key figures were Larkin and O'Brien.

The split in the trade union movement was preceded by a

9. *Ibid.*, 121.
10. *Ibid.*, 126.
11. *Forty-eighth Annual Report of the Irish Trade Union Congress*, 1942, 22.

breakaway from the Labour Party. During the early war years
there had been an upsurge of activity in the Dublin Labour
Party, and branch organization, long moribund, expanded
throughout the city. In December 1941, Jim Larkin was re-
admitted a member of the Labour Party and in the following
year was elected to Dublin Corporation as an official Labour
candidate. It was at the municipal election in 1942 that
Labour in Dublin achieved its greatest electoral success, winning 13 seats out of 35 and becoming the biggest party in the
Corporation.

It was Larkin's membership of the party that led to the
disaffiliation of the Irish Transport and General Workers'
Union, which came about in the following year. Some time
before the general election of 1943, a selection conference of
the Labour Party had nominated Larkin as a candidate for
the Dublin North-East Constituency, but the Administrative
Council had declined to ratify the nomination, by 8 votes to 7,
all 8 members of the I.T.G.W.U. on the Council voting
against the ratification of Larkin's candidature.[12] However,
shortly before the general election took place, the Labour
candidates for Dublin city and county, with one exception,
acting in conjunction with the Dublin Executive of the party,
decided to nominate Larkin as an official Labour candidate.[13]
This decision was accepted by the leader of the party, William
Norton, who spoke with Larkin at election meetings.

Larkin was elected to Dáil Éireann as were three other
Labour deputies in Dublin, bringing the total number of
Labour seats in the Dáil to 17, the party's largest representation since the 'twenties. But this electoral success was soon to
turn bitter.

At the meeting of the Labour Party's Administrative Council held on 3 December 1943, the I.T.G.W.U. members

12. *Official Statement relating to the disaffiliation from the Labour Party of the Irish
Transport and General Workers' Union*, prepared by the Administrative Council
for the information of Party Branches, Divisional and Constituency Councils
and the affiliated Corporate Bodies, 5 February 1944.

13. *Ibid.*

moved the expulsion from the party of the chairman of the Dublin Executive, Deputy James Larkin, junior, and the secretary, on the grounds that in promoting the candidature of Jim Larkin, senior, they had acted in defiance of the Party Constitution. This motion was defeated, the 8 I.T.G.W.U. members voting for it, but all the remaining 9 members voting against it.[14] A fortnight later the I.T.G.W.U. decided to disaffiliate from the Labour Party.

The disaffiliation of the I.T.G.W.U. was promptly followed by the secession of 5 Labour deputies who were members of that union.[15] However, three of their union colleagues, Deputies T. J. Murphy, Richard Corish and Patrick Hogan, remained with the party. In the statement announcing their withdrawal from the parliamentary Labour Party, the 5 deputies implied that they were doing so because of Communist influence in the Labour Party.[16] This also was the main point made in a pamphlet issued over the name of William O'Brien on behalf of the Irish Transport and General Workers' Union which charged that the Labour Party was Communist-dominated, that Communists had taken possession of the party in Dublin, that the Labour Party had allowed the virus of Communism to enter its system too deeply to permit of any hope of recovering its independence and that the leader of the party, William Norton, was fully aware of these facts.[17]

Allegations, exposures, revelations, followed in quick succession, notably in the Dublin weekly newspaper, *The Standard*, which carried a series of articles under such headlines as 'Communist Victory over Irish Labour', 'Story of the Red Coup in the Party'.[18] The wild allegations bandied about in the course of the ensuing controversy may, in retrospect,

14. *Ibid.*
15. These were James Everett, T. D. Looney, John O'Leary, James P. Pattison and Dan Spring.
16. Joint Statement dated 26 January 1944.
17. *Irish Transport and General Workers' Union and the Labour Party. The Union's Reply to the Labour Party's Statement.* Issued for I.T.G.W.U. by William O'Brien, General Secretary, n.d.
18. *The Standard,* 17 March 1944.

appear farcical but they were to have serious political implications for Labour.

In the 1943 general election Labour had gained 8 of the 10 seats that Fianna Fáil lost but in the 1944 election only 8 of the 12 outgoing Labour Party deputies were returned while 4 of the 5 deputies who constituted the National Labour Party, as the breakaway group called itself, were re-elected. The combined Labour and National Labour vote totalled 135,000, a drop of 74,000 or one-third as compared with the 1943 election.

The split in the political Labour movement, notwithstanding the highly-charged accusations of Communist domination of the Labour Party that had been levelled against it by the National Labour Party, was to be effectively healed within a few years. The healing of the breach came about when leaders of both parties joined the Inter-Party government following the 1948 general election. The formal reunion took place in 1950.

The split in the trade union movement was far more serious. Though related to developments in the Labour Party and certainly influenced by the Larkin-O'Brien conflict, the roots of the crisis in the Irish Trade Union Congress lay deeper and were more complex. For many years, leaders of Irish-based and British-based unions had worked uneasily together within the Congress. Conflicts of personality and ambition added to the tensions created by genuinely held differences of opinion on the forms of trade union organization best suited to Irish conditions. One of the complicating factors was that the Congress had covered the whole of Ireland since its foundation in 1894, with British-based unions organizing workers both north and south of the Border. In Northern Ireland, the overwhelming majority of the workers were in British-based unions. At the same time, there was a strong feeling among elements in the Irish-based unions, which were almost wholly confined to the Twenty-Six Counties, that workers should be in Irish unions, a view that was openly supported by the government.

The latent conflict between certain Irish-based unions, par-

ticularly the I.T.G.W.U., and British-based unions, came to a
head towards the end of the war, but on an issue not directly
related to the controversy about Irish-based and British-based
unions. Late in 1943 the British T.U.C. extended to the Irish
T.U.C. an invitation to a World Trade Union Conference to
be held in London. The National Executive was sharply
divided on the question of the acceptance of the invitation
which eventually it declined.[19] At the 1944 Congress held in
Drogheda, Senator Sam Kyle, the leader of the largest British-
based union, the Amalgamated Transport and General
Workers' Union, moved a motion regretting this decision by
the National Executive. In the course of a tense and acrimonious debate, William O'Brien prophesied that if the
motion was passed it would be 'the first step in the break-up
of the Congress'.[20] Those who, like Mr O'Brien, supported the
rejection of the invitation to the London conference, held that
the attendance of Irish delegates would be a breach of Irish
neutrality. In the event, Senator Kyle's motion *was* passed by
96 votes to 73.[21]

The result of the vote on this issue, significant in itself, was
the more so in that it reflected a sharp change in the alignment of forces within the Congress. Whereas the National
Executive elected in 1943 had included 9 members of Irish-
based unions and 6 members of British-based unions, the election at the 1944 Congress resulted in a reversal of these
figures, 9 of the members of the new National Executive being
from British-based unions and only 6 from Irish-based unions.
In accordance with the decision taken by the Congress this
new Executive appointed 2 of its members, Deputy Michael
Keyes and Gilbert Lynch, to attend the London Conference
which was held in February 1945, that is, just a few months
before the war ended.

Shortly afterwards, on 21 March 1945, a conference of 15
Irish-based unions including the Irish Transport and General

19. *Fiftieth Annual Report of the Irish Trade Union Congress*, 1944, 35.
20. *Ibid.*, 106.
21. *Ibid.*, 115–6.

Workers' Union, decided that 'the opinions and aspirations of Irish Labour cannot be expressed by the Irish T.U.C.' which it alleged was 'controlled by British Trade Unions'. The conference recommended withdrawal from the Congress and the establishment of an organization composed of trade unions with headquarters in Ireland.[22] On 25 April 1945, the Congress of Irish Unions was formally established.[23]

Lengthy manifestoes issued by the two Congresses set out their respective positions on the issues involved. The Irish T.U.C. declared that the issue was democracy or dictatorship.[24] No border of geography or creed had been recognized by the Congress, which had been a unifying force in the country, a living symbol of the ultimate unity of the Irish people. It stressed the international traditions of the trade union movement, interpreted the breakaway as a new partition in which the workers of the North were to be excluded from participation in the Irish trade union movement and in which the workers in the Twenty-Six Counties were also to be divided. The Irish T.U.C. rejected the allegation that it was controlled by British-based unions. At no time for 30 years, it said, had these unions sent sufficient delegates to Congress to give them a majority. At the 1944 Congress, in fact, the British-based unions had fewer delegates than the Irish-based unions, yet their affiliated membership was far greater.

The Congress of Irish Unions in its manifesto took its stand upon the fundamental principle of the right of the Irish people to be complete masters of their own destinies.[25] It proclaimed the right and duty of Irish trade unionists to organize in their own Irish trade unions and pledged itself to put an end to the domination of British unions. It denounced the

22. See *A History of the Foundation of Comhar Ceárd Éireann,* (Congress of Irish Unions), 1946, 16.

23. *Ibid.,* 17.

24. *Democracy or Dictatorship? The Irish Trade Union Congress Appeals to the Workers of Ireland,* issued by the National Executive of the Irish T.U.C., 24 May 1945.

25. *To the Trade Unionists of Ireland,* issued on behalf of the Provisional Committee of Congress of Irish Unions, 27 June 1945.

sending of delegates to the London conference which it said 'had brought to a head and into the open the irreconcilable differences on British unions in Ireland'. The C.I.U. manifesto called on Irish unions to associate with it and urged Irish members of British unions to join existing Irish unions or to organize new Irish unions. Both manifestoes had recourse to James Connolly's writings in support of their respective positions.

From 1945, therefore, there were two rival Congresses in existence. The Irish T.U.C. with both Irish-based and British-based unions in affiliation, represented the great majority of trade unionists in the country as a whole. It included 15 Irish-based unions, among them the Workers' Union of Ireland, which now after years in the wilderness was accepted into the Congress, and almost all the British-based unions. The Congress of Irish Unions on the other hand consisted of 16 Irish-based unions, including the I.T.G.W.U., and its membership was almost wholly confined to the Twenty-Six Counties.

It will be evident that the background to the divisions in the political Labour movement and in the trade union movement was involved and complicated. It is not easy to unravel the tangled skeins. A key factor clearly was the position and role of the Irish Transport and General Workers' Union within the Labour movement and in particular the influence of its general secretary, William O'Brien. The long-standing feud between O'Brien and Larkin, which had persisted over the 20 years since Larkin's return from America, was also an important element in the situation. These two antagonists were men of sharply contrasting stamp. The daemonic force in Larkin which had been so manifest during the 1913 struggle had nothing in common with the reserved character of O'Brien.

Larkin's turbulent personality and volatile temperament contrasted with O'Brien's cold and calculating astuteness. O'Brien had displayed thoroughness and administrative talent in building up the membership and finances of the

Irish Transport and General Workers' Union. His insistence on system, method, regulations tended to obscure from his colleagues and his critics a sharp and subtle mind. An acute observer has described him as being 'beyond doubt one of the keenest minds and most efficient organizers any movement has produced in the country in the last 40 years'.[26] But there is no doubt of his deep and abiding hostility to Larkin.

Early in 1946 William O'Brien retired as general secretary of the Irish Transport and General Workers' Union and just a year later Larkin died. But the split persisted.

Various attempts were made to bring the two Congresses together, by William Norton, by Seán Lemass and, most dramatically perhaps, by Deputy Jim Larkin, junior, in an historic open letter written on the day that James Larkin was laid to rest.[27] He wrote,

> The great mass of working men and women who con-
> stitute the Irish Labour Movement must ardently desire
> that their strength and purpose should be added to a
> thousandfold, by all that flows from unity . . . Irish
> people are emotional and perhaps our common emotion
> this day may give us that unity we need, where reason
> and argument have failed in the past.
>
> I have no doubt of the truth of my statement when
> I declare that unity is the single quality sought for by
> the working men and women who constitute and who
> are the Irish Labour Movement, and why therefore
> when so little stands between them and the unity they
> desire should they be denied it?

The division, however, endured, a source of much conten-
tion among the trade unions, weakening their influence and
stultifying their development, and creating great difficulties

26. Profile of William O'Brien in *The Leader*, 31 January 1953.
27. Published in *The Irish Times*, 5 February 1947.

in industrial relations. Ironically, while the trade union movement entered the post-war period weakened by disunity and dissension, the main employers' organization emerged strengthened and united. The Federated Union of Employers, which under its former name of the Dublin Employers' Federation went back to 1911—formed then to combat Larkin's activities—had been registered in 1941 under the Trade Union Act and had rapidly expanded its organization among employers.

The end of the war and the impending lifting of the emergency control of wages that had been in operation since 1941 would, it was feared, give rise to bitter industrial conflict as the trade unions sought to recover the ground lost during the period of control. In an endeavour to avert such conflict or at least diminish it, the Minister for Industry and Commerce, Mr Seán Lemass, introduced in 1946 the Industrial Relations Bill. This was largely an agreed measure, accepted by both Congresses and by the employers' organizations. Under it was set up the Labour Court, an independent body on which workers and employers had equal representation and whose recommendations were not binding but could be accepted or rejected by the parties to disputes. Under the firm chairmanship of R. J. P. Mortished, the Court quickly assumed an important role in industrial relations and achieved considerable success in mediation and conciliation in disputes. The first worker members of the Court, the Labour leaders, Thomas Johnson and Cathal O'Shannon, ensured trade union confidence, and a very high proportion of the Court's recommendations were accepted by the workers. This development in industrial relations—the first significant development in this area of affairs since the establishment of the state—certainly reduced the incidence of industrial strife even if it was not always successful in averting strikes.

The Labour Court was also instrumental in bringing about an important new departure in wage negotiations. It was under its auspices that what was in effect the first National

Wage Agreement was formulated in 1948—the eleven shilling-formula agreement as it was called.[28]

Turning again to industry, the early post-war period was to see a remarkable expansion in both production and employment in the industrial sector. Neither before nor since has industry achieved as rapid a rate of growth as it did then. By 1946 the volume of industrial production had about recovered its pre-war level. Over the next five years it increased by two thirds.[29] Employment in industry also grew rapidly and 62,000 new industrial jobs were provided between 1946 and 1951.[30] While there was rapid expansion over the whole of industry, building in particular showed a spectacular increase due in large part to the intensified housing drive initiated by the Inter-Party government.

In 1949 the Industrial Development Authority was set up with Dr James Beddy, one of the architects of Ireland's industrial expansion programme, as chairman. Not only was this Authority to be a promotional body encouraging and assisting industrial development but it was also intended that it should initiate proposals for new industries. Its efforts were to lead to the establishment of many important industrial projects.

By 1951 about 22 per cent of the working population were engaged in industry compared with 17 per cent before the war.[31] A sizeable industrial sector was now in existence but despite a rapid post-war expansion, many weaknesses in its structure and organization were apparent. Industry continued to be highly protected. Insufficient efforts were made to ensure that it was efficient, while the general level of managerial competence remained mediocre. Production was still geared almost wholly to home consumption, little progress having been made in developing new industrial exports. These were some of the factors that were to halt industrial expansion and cause virtual stagnation in industrial employment throughout the 'fifties.

28. *Second Annual Report of the Labour Court,* 1948.
29. *Statistical Abstract,* 1956, table 98.
30. *Ibid.,* table 35.
31. *Ibid.*

Church and State in Modern Ireland

R. Dudley Edwards

Fears for the future, founded in nightmares about the past, be-devilled the new-born Irish states.

The 1920 partition of Ireland severed, politically, the predominantly Catholic, from the predominantly Protestant, parts of the country. Ecclesiastically, however, the 32 counties were not partitioned. The minority Church in each area depended for stability on the neighbouring area in which it had more predominance.

The situation at the beginning of 1922, however, was far from clear. The recently-signed articles of agreement for a treaty under which the Irish Free State was to be set up appeared to contravene the partition arrangements of the Government of Ireland Act of 1920. Few people favouring self-government in the Nationalist tradition believed that two separate states would be maintained. The Catholic hierarchy had, for some time, been involved in the national struggle. They had condemned conscription in 1918 at the instance of the Nationalist Parties. They had protested against British misgovernment throughout 1920 and also against the Belfast pogroms which continued into 1922. In these circumstances, it appeared but natural for the hierarchy to express their views on the treaty, as indeed did nearly every other politically conscious group in the country.

It is true that the hierarchy expressed themselves particularly quickly on the treaty and in fact before a vote had been taken upon it by Dáil Éireann. Very soon afterwards, Pope Benedict XV, practically as his last public act before his death, expressed his satisfaction at the agreement, both to King George V and to the Irish people. In the months which followed, the bishops continued to be concerned in their public pronouncements about the dangers of civil war, as well as the impropriety of partition. Gradually, it began to emerge that, in fact, they were aware of their strong position as the leaders of the Church of more than 93 per cent of the population of the Twenty-Six Counties. And because of the extent to which their support had been relied upon in the long political struggle, they felt in a strong position to exert influence at this time. It would be true to say, however, that they were acting, as they had always done in the nineteenth century, with the knowledge that they were sanctioning the view of the majority of Catholics who at the time were weary of war and wanted peace.

There is no doubt that several of the bishops did their utmost to prevent the outbreak of civil war, but once this began, they came down heavily on the side of the provisional government and of the new Dáil Éireann Executive set up after the endorsement of the treaty. In this they felt justified as at the general election, just before the outbreak of civil war, the pro-treaty candidates had proved successful in far greater numbers than had their opponents. When, therefore, in October 1922, they issued a joint pastoral on the Civil War, they took their stand upon the popular endorsement at the election, much to the dissatisfaction of the republicans whose view it was that the bishops had no right to treat the Republic as disestablished.

The bishops regarded the provisional government as the lawfully constituted government of the country. It therefore followed that the republican forces were engaged in the subversion of the sole lawfully constituted authority; that their actions against the forces of the state lacked all moral justification and that they were indulging in murder, robbery and other criminal acts.

The Republic, however, in the view of the anti-treaty minority, was not disestablished. A few days after the pastoral had been read in the churches on 22 October 1922, de Valera, having secretly convened the anti-treaty members of the second Dáil, established an emergency government which claimed to be the *de jure* government of the country. He appealed to Rome against the action of the bishops and an informal papal representative, Monsignor Luzio, was sent to Ireland to report on the situation. The government of the Free State had, in the meantime, on 6 December 1922, come into existence and set up the machinery of the new state. Republicans now found themselves liable to a denial of the sacraments particularly at the hands of the diocesan clergy. Considerable resentment against the bishops followed, but it is notable that, unlike revolutionary movements in other parts of Europe, no anti-clerical party, as such, developed in Ireland though there remained a certain residual anti-episcopal feeling among many anti-treaty leaders. This was not entirely without consequence for relations between Church and State when Mr de Valera and an anti-treaty group eventually came to power.

The relations of Church and State as laid down in the Constitution of 1922 should be compared with the arrangements set forth in the Constitution of 1937. The relevant articles differ substantially in tone. In the Free State Constitution, article 8 reads as follows :

> Freedom of conscience and the free profession and practice of religion are, subject to public order and morality, guaranteed to every citizen, and no law may be made either directly or indirectly to endow any religion, or prohibit or restrict the free exercise thereof or give any preference, or impose any disability on account of religious belief or religious status, or affect prejudicially the right of any child to attend a school receiving public money without attending the religious instruction at the

school, or make any discrimination as respects State aid between schools under the management of different religious denominations, or divert from any religious denomination or any educational institution any of its property except for the purpose of roads, railways, lighting, water or drainage works or other works of public utility, and on payment of compensation.

But article 44 of the 1937 Constitution states:

I.   1.   The State acknowledges that the homage of public worship is due to Almighty God. It shall hold His Name in reverence, and shall respect and honour religion.

2.   The State recognizes the special position of the Holy Catholic Apostolic and Roman Church as the guardian of the faith professed by the great majority of the citizens.

3.   The State also recognizes the Church of Ireland, the Presbyterian Church in Ireland, the Methodist Church in Ireland, the Religious Society of Friends in Ireland, as well as the Jewish Congregations and the other religious denominations existing in Ireland at the date of the coming into operation of this Constitution.

———————

II.   1.   Freedom of conscience and the free profession and practice of religion are, subject to public order and morality, guaranteed to every citizen.

2.   The State guarantees not to endow any religion.

3.   The State shall not impose any disabilities or make any discrimination on the ground of religious profession, belief or status.

4. Legislation providing State aid for schools shall not discriminate between schools under the management of different religious denominations, nor be such as to affect prejudicially the right of any child to attend a school receiving public money without attending religious instruction at that school.

5. Every religious denomination shall have the right to manage its own affairs, own, acquire, and administer property, movable and immovable, and maintain religious institutions for religious and charitable purposes.

6. The property of any religious denomination or any educational institution shall not be diverted save for necessary works of public utility and on payment of compensation.

———

The Free State version was secular in flavour and had no necessarily Catholic or indeed Christian bias. It might have been drafted by an agnostic liberal anywhere in the world. The 1937 Constitution bears a distinctively Catholic and Irish flavour. It is well known that some of its social paragraphs were written with the assistance of a prominent Catholic ecclesiastic. On the drafting of article 44, leaders of other religious communities were consulted.

It is difficult to say if this difference of tone has had any real significance for the practical relationship of Church and state before and after 1937. One point of great importance in the history of that relationship has been the absence of Church leaders from the legislature. Mr Cosgrave's government had seen to it that no bishop became a member of the upper house as happened in so many other countries. This reflected, as did the Constitution of 1937, the separation of Church and state—a traditional factor in Ireland since the disestablishment of the Protestant episcopal Church. There is no evidence, indeed, that Church authorities sought such representation. There is some irony in the fact that the party which framed the first Constitution, secular as it may have sounded on religious matters, has generally seemed to have been more amenable to ecclesiastical pressure, publicly and privately, than was Fianna Fáil, whose leader was responsible for the drafting of the second and more emphatically Christian document.

The 1937 Constitution also recognized the special position of the family as a social unit. It prohibited the passing of any legislation permitting divorce and it incorporated the principle that there existed a special obligation to make provision for the family so as not to require the employment of mothers of families outside of their homes.

This Constitution, some twenty years later, was praised by Pope Pius XII for its manifestation of Catholic and Christian principles.

Other matters increasingly interested ecclesiastical groups in Ireland. The case in favour of literary and film censorship was expressed very clearly, quite early in the 1920s. It began to emerge that in the Twenty-Six Counties Church elements recognized the significance of these and related issues. They took action to influence the Free State government against the approval of any bill to permit divorce. In consequence of a report presented by a government-appointed committee on evil literature, they were able to influence the introduction and passage of the Censorship Act, which set up a permanent board to prohibit literature advocating birth control or publications considered to be obscene or indecent. In the same period, the first steps were taken to influence public opinion against Communism, in continuation of the older warnings against secret societies and international conspiracies. In the same period, too, there was a reiteration of the traditional Irish Catholic position against non-Catholic schools, including Trinity College, Dublin.

From 1925, it was clear that partition between Northern

Ireland and the Irish Free State had come to stay at least for some considerable time and on the existing boundary between the Six Counties and the Twenty-Six. The bishops whose jurisdictions were in Northern Ireland or mainly within that territory became increasingly concerned about local conditions and particularly the operation of the education acts in the North, which made it more difficult to maintain the denominational system which had emerged during the nineteenth century. Under the new Northern Ireland government, described by its Prime Minister, Lord Craigavon, as a Protestant government for a Protestant people, there emerged a new state-endowed system of education in contrast to which the denominationally organized schools secured considerably less support. Most of the Protestant communities made terms with the Northern state, thus having the best of both worlds. In this situation, the contrast with the position in the South was not favourable from the standpoint of Catholic ecclesiastics. There was undoubtedly some qualification in the minds of many Catholic managers and reserves in particular on the policy of increasingly teaching through Irish, but the system in the Free State secured Catholic support, in consequence of the contrast.

So far, little has been said of any Church except the Roman Catholic as the various Protestant Churches and other religious communities together amounted to such a small number in the Irish Free State. Among them, the same reservation about the intensification of Irish teaching existed, but otherwise these communities appeared to be satisfied with their position. Relations between the Catholic Church and these other communities improved. On one occasion, early in the 1920s, the leaders of the major Churches in the Belfast area combined in an appeal to terminate the pogroms. This had, however, little long-term effect.

From the entry into the Dáil in 1927 of Fianna Fáil, a substantial number of the Catholic clergy expressed themselves publicly in favour of President Cosgrave and against the new republican party. The first beginnings, however, of a new episcopal attitude to Mr de Valera emerged with the consecration in 1924 of Bishop John Duignan of Clonfert. From that time there was no longer a monolithic ecclesiastical attitude towards republicanism. The assassination of Kevin O'Higgins in the summer of 1927 did produce further condemnations of secret societies and created a certain amount of anti-clerical resentment among republicans who insisted that these pronouncements were directed against the new constitutional movement. In the years that followed until 1932, social unrest spread in Ireland as elsewhere in the world in consequence of the Great Depression. The rise in unemployment and the fear of Socialism and of Communism became increasingly expressed in episcopal pronouncements.

In the autumn of 1931, a collective episcopal pastoral condemned Saor Éire, a republican organization with a socialistic policy, and also, an unnamed body described as being of a militant nature. In the subsequent general election, the forces of Fianna Fáil and Labour secured sufficient votes to defeat Mr Cosgrave who was replaced as President of the Executive Council by Mr de Valera. This was the beginning of a 16-year period of office for Fianna Fáil. Mr de Valera, on the occasion of the visit to Ireland of Cardinal Lorenzo Lauri, for the Eucharistic Congress in 1932, expressed his belief that ten years' misunderstanding between the Church and republicanism had now happily come to an end. This was to prove correct for most purposes but the suspicion of churchmen, and of bishops in particular, towards republicanism and Socialism continued to be demonstrated.

Mr de Valera's foreign policy was often in conflict with what appeared to be the attitude of various ecclesiastics and particular groups of the Catholic laity. These did not necessarily represent the Church but they did represent an average Catholic viewpoint. For example, Mr de Valera was very strong in his support of the League of Nations, an organization from which the papacy had been excluded at its foundation. He advocated the acceptance of Soviet Russia's request to be admitted into the League. He supported the imposition of sanctions on the Catholic state of Italy over its invasion of Abyssinia in 1935-6. He did this at a time when the Italian hierarchy gave its enthusiastic support to Mussolini's invasion. The Pope himself on one notable occasion had seemingly added his authority in justification of that enterprise. Mr de Valera also delayed recognition of General Franco's government for a very long time—until indeed the Spanish Republican government had ceased to enforce effective *de facto* authority over the greater part of Spain. This Mr de Valera did, despite strong attacks from the opposition which desired the recognition of a Catholic government as against a 'red regime'. An Irish Christian Front had been mobilized in Ireland to support by armed force General Franco's cause in Spain. Church door collections were taken and most ecclesiastics were assumed to countenance these pro-Franco activities. No direct pressure was brought to bear by churchmen but indirect pressure was there, however sporadic and ineffective. There was, in fact, no Church-state collision on this issue.

During the years of the Second World War, the Catholic hierarchy in Ireland became more closely associated with the state over the policy of neutrality, and new faces replaced old on the bench of bishops. In particular, Cardinal MacRory expressed himself in this way. After the ratification of the Constitution, he had early in 1938 praised it publicly. On the outbreak of war, he became concerned about the question of conscription. His feelings against partition were expressed upon numerous occasions and there is little doubt that he believed that partition could only be terminated by a German victory. He was careful, however, to follow the general policy of Mr de Valera who supported him on the question of protesting against compulsory military service being imposed in Northern Ireland. The position of the Cardinal was unhesitatingly expressed as being based upon the forcible exclusion of the Northern Catholics from the rest of the country and on the moral objection to their being compelled to fight for Britain. The Primate's position, however, was somewhat different to that of other bishops, but, in general, his attitude helped to achieve a closer accord with Mr de Valera's government in the South.

At the end of the war, various schemes for social legislation became increasingly popular. Dr Duignan of Clonfert put forward a social benefits scheme which was remarkable in its day as being 20 years ahead of current economic thinking. Largely under the influence of Mr MacEntee, the government decided not to adopt the Duignan scheme. A Health Act introduced in 1947 came under some criticism from the medical profession and gained some indirect endorsement from some of the bishops but it was not until after Mr de Valera left office in 1948, that disagreement between Church and state on social issues emerged in a major way.

The government which took office after the defeat of Mr de Valera was formed under the leadership of Mr John A. Costello, and it was an Inter-Party coalition. Immediately after his election, Mr Costello expressed himself in old-fashioned diplomatic phraseology in an address to the Pope in which he stated the intention of passing social legislation based upon Catholic principles. The subsequent public health bill, colloquially known as the 'mother and child' scheme, was condemned at a meeting of the hierarchy as an undue invasion of the rights of the individual and as a potential danger to Catholic principles regarding sex, marriage, birth-control and pre-natal care. This was followed by the defeat of the government at a general election after which Mr de Valera returned to office. A new Public Health Bill was evolved, a formula based on a nominal contribution being devised to meet objections to the previous bill. It would appear that Mr de Valera secured acceptance of his policy by observing a more detached diplomacy with the hierarchy and so a period came to an end in which, except for this one major matter, the relations of Church and state were amicable. It must be said, however, that Northern Protestant Unionist propaganda made full use of the 'mother and child' controversy to stress the view that the influence of Rome was exercised in a secret and indirect manner upon the government of the Twenty-Six Counties.

Reviewing the relations of the Catholic Church and the state at the end of this particular generation, it is clear that the position accorded to the Church in the Constitution of 1937 was no mere fiction. In the realm of law, in several instances, the discipline of the Church was upheld in reversal of decisions taken in post-Reformation England, so that the law binding members of the Church was admitted in evidence, though there was no alteration in the existing law of the land, where a conflict arose on interpretations of circumstances justifying the nullification of marriage. The growing strength of Catholicism is also evident from the remarkable increase in the number of persons following a religious vocation. In the case of members of the Orders, there was more than double the number in 1951 as compared with 1921. The increase was not so great, however, in the case of secular clergy, though a 25 per cent increase is quite considerable. The number of houses of religious, including nuns, also increased by at least 25 per cent. Paralleling this development, of course, must be noted the general increase in prosperity in the country, and the substantial decrease of poverty. In conclusion, it may be said that there was an atmosphere of quietness which reflected the strength as well as the security tinged sometimes with complacency, which the Church enjoyed in modern Ireland.

E

The Changing Pattern of Irish
Society, 1938-51

GERARD   QUINN

In the fifteen years between 1936 and 1951, there was no great change either in the total population of the country or in the working population. Both showed slight decreases. But there was a very considerable change in the type of work done. The numbers engaged in agriculture dropped by about 109,000 persons while the numbers employed in industry increased by about 96,000. At the start of this period about half of the total working population were in agriculture—at its end, only two in every five workers were in farming.[1]

DECLINING FARMING POPULATION

There was nothing new or exceptional in this trend towards a diminishing farm population and a shift from agricultural to industrial employment. It was a trend which had existed for many years previously and which has continued until the present time. It was a trend also experienced in many other countries. But there were—and are—some unique features of the Irish experience which made it a good deal less socially acceptable.

In most other countries the change from agriculture to industry took place in the context of increasing total employment, with the expansion of industry outpacing the

1. Throughout this essay the statistical references are to the Twenty-Six Counties area only.

120

decline in agriculture. It took place also in the context of an increasing total population. But in Ireland both the total and the working populations remained static. Another way of expressing the same point—in other countries the change predominantly represented migration within the country, while in Ireland it was accompanied by heavy emigration out of the country.

The Census of Population Reports of 1946 and 1951 show some important differences between the periods to which they refer. In the ten years up to 1946 the yearly average decline in the numbers at work in farming was 4,400. This was broadly in line with the experience of the previous ten years.

However, in the immediate post-war period there was a very heavy acceleration in the outflow from agriculture. Between 1946 and 1951 the average annual outflow was 14,200—a rate of decline more than three times heavier than in the previous twenty years.

Also, in the ten years up to 1946, more women than men left work on the land. The proportionate decline in the case of women was exceptionally high—little short of one quarter, while the proportionate drop for men was about 4 per cent.

In the post-war period the balance between men and women in the flow from agriculture was decisively reversed. Men comprised no less than 87 per cent of the total decline. The annual rate of decline for men was very nearly six times heavier than in the previous ten years.

Between 1946 and 1951 the loss of members of farming families was very nearly as great as for the whole of the previous twenty years. The drop in the number of farm labourers was four times greater than in the previous twenty years.

Another interesting difference between these two periods is that up to 1946, the drop in men at work in agriculture was completely concentrated in farms of under 30 acres with the vast majority in the under 15-acre category. Between 1946 and 1951, the fall in men was widely spread over all sizes of farms with each size losing broadly the same proportion of its male workers.

In the post-war period, therefore, there was an astonishingly rapid acceleration in the number of men leaving agriculture and the habit of leaving the land spread from the very small farms to all sizes of farms.

EMIGRATION

Emigration throughout this period was heavy. Between 1936 and 1946, the emigration figure was 18,700 persons a year; between 1946 and 1951 it increased to 24,300 a year. This steep increase of about 30 per cent in the emigration rate was brought about entirely by a very rapid acceleration in the number of women emigrating in the immediate post-war period, when the annual rate of female emigration almost doubled to over 14,000 a year.

Emigration took its heaviest toll in the rural areas. In this period, Munster was the province with the greatest volume of emigration, but the province with the highest rate of emigration—that is, as measured per 1,000 of population—was Connacht. Between 1936 and 1946, among the counties with the highest emigration rates were Leitrim, Cavan, Kerry and Longford. This bears out one of the fundamental features of Irish emigration. It has been heaviest in those counties which have a high proportion of small and poor farms, a relatively small town population, and a high concentration of population living on farms and in small villages.

DESTINATION OF EMIGRANTS

A decisive change in the destination of emigrants began from the mid-'thirties onwards. The preponderance of the United Kingdom in present emigration sometimes obscures the fact that, up till the mid-1930s, the United States was the country chosen by the great majority of Irish emigrants.

In the ten years up to 1936, well over half of total emigration was to the United States. But after 1936, emigration was mainly to the United Kingdom. In the seven years before the outbreak of war, emigration to countries other than Britain was more than offset by emigrants returning under the impact of the Great Depression. In the war years emigration to North America was negligible. However, emigration to the United Kingdom increased dramatically from the mid-'thirties onwards so that the total emigration rate proceeded much as before.

There is detailed information about the occupations and ages of emigrants to the United Kingdom between 1940 and 1951, supplied from travel documents and identity cards. The great majority of emigrants, both men and women, were young and came from the poorest sections of the population. Almost half the men who received travel documents were under the age of 25; two thirds were under the age of 30. Women emigrants were even younger; seven in every ten were under 25 years of age. There was also a progressive tendency towards younger emigration. In this eleven-year period the proportion of men emigrants over the age of 30 dropped steadily, while the proportion aged between 16 and 24 increased from 33 per cent to 55 per cent. A similar trend was discernible in the case of women emigrants. The Commission on Emigration and Other Population Problems, which was set up by Mr William Norton under the chairmanship of Dr J. P. Beddy and reported in 1954, is a definitive analysis of this period of Irish economic and social history. The Commission attributed the tendency towards younger emigration to the fact that emigration to the United Kingdom, unlike previous emigration to the United States, was not regarded as involving the same permanent break with country and family.

Approximately three quarters of the men who received travel documents described their last occupation as that of unskilled labourer, builder's labourer or farm worker; more than half of the women described themselves as domestic workers. Unskilled workers with a predominantly rural background dominated Irish emigration in this period; throughout the 1950s there was an increase in the number of emigrants possessing a skill, whether a technical or a professional qualification. Even though Irish emigrants were mainly from rural areas, they tended to settle in the larger cities in their country of adoption. According to the 1940 Population Census in the United States nine out of every ten Irish emigrants were living in towns and cities and more than half were living in five major cities—New York, Chicago, Philadelphia, Boston and San Francisco. The 1951 Population Census in Britain showed the same picture. One third of Irish emigrants in England and Wales were living in the Greater London area; in Scotland, 40 per cent of emigrants from Ireland were living in Glasgow.

It appeared that not only did Irish emigrants change their country; they also changed from rural life to city life and very largely from farm work to unskilled work in industry in their country of adoption.

Emigration, then as now, was the result of a number of influences, social and economic:—the conditions of poverty that existed on the small uneconomic farms; the underemployment of members of farming families; the lack of alternative employment opportunities; the poor marriage prospects; the lack of social intercourse that made country life dull and unsatisfying. Set against these economic and social defects of Irish country life was the opportunity, easily availed of, of a better life—at least in the material sense—that offered across the Channel. It was not only the very poor and the under-employed who took the emigrant boat. As awareness of the availability and conditions of industrial life in Britain grew, many left Ireland to seek a better life who were far from being on the subsistence level in their homeland. Proximity, ease of travel, absence of language barrier, frequently a family connection already in England—all acted to encourage emigration.

Emigration meant that those who stayed in Ireland as well

as those who left, enjoyed a higher standard of living than if the nation had to support the natural increase of its population over these years. If emigration had not existed, in the post-war period especially, a sharp reduction in living standards and a severe unemployment problem would have been inevitable. Irish national output was increasing at a negligible rate, far lower than that of other countries. At a time when living standards elsewhere, and especially in Britain, were increasing rapidly under the impetus of post-war recovery, it may be questioned whether the Irish community would have been willing to acquiesce in a growing disparity between their living standards and those elsewhere.

In this sense emigration cannot readily be described as a conclusive sign of national decay, as it has often been presented. Nonetheless, it did exact its price. In purely economic terms it meant a static or declining market which provided a poor environment for investment, initiative, production and employment. But more than this, emigration, when it is as persistent and deep-rooted a feature of the nation's life as it was in Ireland, introduces a sense of social malaise, a lack of national self-confidence, the pessimistic mood inevitable in a nation which feels itself unable to provide for its people. This is an intangible factor but it is perhaps the gravest consequence of heavy continuing emigration.

The Irish population was an ageing one. In an international comparison of twenty-five countries, made by the Emigration Commission, the Republic had the lowest proportion of its population in the age group between 15 and 44, which may be taken as representing the active working section. At the same time we had the highest proportion, with one exception, in the over-65 grouping. This was largely a consequence of emigration which, over many years, has had its greatest impact on the younger section of the population.

The result was to leave Ireland with an abnormally high 'dependency' ratio. In 1951, two in every five of the entire population were under 14 or over 65 years of age—the highest proportion, by a considerable margin, of all the 25 countries surveyed. A number of implications flow from this fact. The burden on the working section of the population, in supporting the dependency groups either directly within the family or through taxation for matters like education and pensions, tends to be high; the sacrifices involved are greater than elsewhere. Another inevitable consequence of a high proportion of elderly people, which was noted by the Commission, is the permeation of a conservative bias throughout society, barriers to innovations in attitudes and policies—a force which is not measurable in any statistical sense, but is important nonetheless.

Between 1936 and 1951, the biggest proportionate change occurred in the 15 to 44 age grouping. It fell to 41 per cent in the latter year, its lowest level in a century. It is also a striking fact that in the 1951 population of about 3 million there were actually 117,000 more people over 65 than 100 years before, when the total population was more than twice as big.

Fortunately, there is evidence that this long-rooted tendency towards an ageing population is now in process of being reversed. A recent demographic forecast by Dr C. E. V. Leser, of the Economic and Social Research Institute, estimates that the total population in the present decade will increase by about 100,000. More significant still is the estimate that there will be an increase of around 150,000 in the number of persons between the ages of 15 and 30, and an increase of 10,000 in the number of persons under the age of 15.

The 1966 Census of Population disclosed an increase in population of 62,411 or 2.2 per cent. This was a welcome break with long-established trends. Each Census since 1841— with the single exception of 1951, which showed a small increase of 5,481—had indicated a decline in population.

URBANIZATION

Although the total population remained much the same, there was a considerable change in its geographical distribution. This largely reflected the change from agricultural to industrial employm nt. New industries tended to grow up around the principa sea ports and this contributed to a shift in population to Leinster, and, in particular, to the extremely rapid growth of the capital city. By 1951, the population of Leinster was very nearly as big as that of Munster and Connacht combined.

There was a continuing increase in the proportion of the population living in cities and towns. This shift towards town living had been going on since 1841, when only 15 per cent of the population lived in towns—towns in this context meaning a minimum population of 1,500. In the early 'twenties, just one third of the population lived in towns; by 1951, two out of every five of the population did so. A similar tendency towards an increasing proportion of town dwellers was experienced by practically every European country. But there was one important difference. In Ireland the change in the balance of town and rural population was caused mainly by a very heavy fall in the rural population. In other countries the change was brought about by a rapid growth of town populations. However, in Ireland, with the marked exception of Dublin, the growth in other Irish cities and towns in this period was very moderate.

The population of County Dublin increased by 106,000 or nearly one third in this period. This increase was almost entirely caused by the expansion of the Dublin city area. The 1951 Census showed that about one third of the residents of County Dublin were born outside the county, which is a measure of the emigration into Dublin from the rest of the country.

The growth in the Dublin city area was in very sharp contrast to other Irish towns and cities. Yet the growth in the population of Dublin was quite normal by comparison with the major cities of other countries. What was disquieting was not the absolute rate of growth of Dublin, but rather the lack of balance brought about by the failure of other cities and towns in Ireland to grow at anything like the same rate and the depopulation of the countryside. In other countries the pattern was one of increasing total populations, associated with the static or slowly decreasing rural populations and rapid expansion of cities and towns. In Ireland, the total population was static, there was a heavy decline in rural population and, apart from the isolated exception of the capital, relatively little growth in the population of other cities and towns.

The marked change in occupational pattern and distribution which occurred in this period was not just an economic phenomenon; it had important social and political implications. As the emphasis changed from the traditional self-sufficient farming society to an industrially employed community, greater attention had naturally to be paid to social problems such as care of the aged, provision for sickness, and compensation for unemployment. Politically the fall in the rural population was to affect the balance of rural and urban numerical representation in the Dáil; it obviously also made the 'city' vote correspondingly more important.

THE MARRIAGE RATE

Throughout this period the Irish marriage rate was among the lowest in the world. During the war years the number of marriages was around 17,000 each year, while in the post-war period the number remained fairly stable at around 16,000 a year. This represented a marriage rate ranging between 5 and 6 per 1,000 of the population—by far the lowest in a list of 22 countries presented in the Emigration Commission Report. This was not a new trend. An unusually low marriage rate was a feature of Irish society since marriage statistics were first compiled in 1864. The Emigration Commission indeed identified the low rate of marriage as one of the two great population problems facing the country, the other being emigration.

Apart from the unusually low marriage rate, the Irish

marriage pattern disclosed some other uniquely unfavourable features. The average age of marriage was unusually high : in the late 1940s it was 28 years for women, and 33 years for men. The proportion of people marrying in the younger age groupings did show an increase in this period; but, despite this improvement, the percentage of unmarried persons among the younger age groups, and the proportion of persons who never married at all, remained exceedingly high by international standards. The proportion of single men between the ages of 25 and 34 years in 1951 was more than 65 per cent, and the proportion of single women, 45 per cent. The proportion of unmarried people over the age of 55 was 28 per cent for men and 25 per cent for women. Thus, the ratio of people remaining permanently single in the Irish population was about 1 in 4.

There were important variations in marriage pattern between different parts of the country. The number of marriages was relatively greatest in the larger cities and towns. It was much higher in Leinster than in the other provinces. The marriage rate was lowest in Connacht and the three Ulster counties.

There was a significant 'marriage gap' as between the urban and rural populations. The proportion remaining single in the towns was much lower than in rural areas at every age grouping. Part of the reason for this discrepancy between town and countryside was the extremely low ratio of women to men in the rural areas. Ireland as a whole had the unusual experience of having a male majority in its population. This was a phenomenon that first appeared in 1911. In 1951, single men exceeded women by about 50,000, but there was a marked difference in the male/female ratio as between towns and rural areas. The number of women exceeded men by a wide margin in the towns while the reverse applied throughout the countryside. Marriage prospects in the rural areas were obviously affected by this imbalance in the male/female population. But this was probably not a major cause of the marked phenomenon in rural Ireland of low marriage rate, late age of marriage and the very high number of persons remaining single. Despite the pronounced female minority, there were still substantial numbers of unmarried women in the rural areas. The real reasons went a good deal deeper and derived essentially from the social and economic structure of rural life in Ireland.

Contrary to the popular impression, the proportion of farmers marrying was relatively high. In 1946, for example, 72 per cent of all farmers were married, in contrast with a figure of 45 per cent for all occupied males. However, apart from farmers, the proportion remaining unmarried among other male workers in the farming population, that is, the sons who helped on the family farm and the farm employees, was far higher than in other occupations.

Despite the decrease in the number of farmers' sons who remained to assist on the farm in this period, the number still remained high, and the proportion of farmers' sons who remained single was also extremely high. The highest unmarried rate of all was among farm employees. The housing difficulty was a particular impediment to marriage among these groups. The Emigration Commission pointed out that rented flats or rooms were virtually unobtainable in rural areas. Often outright purchase of a house was the only alternative, and this amounted to an impassable barrier against marriage prospects for the relatively poor sections of the farming population. Clearly, too, the low marriage rate and high emigration from rural Ireland were intimately connected. The poorness of marriage prospects tended to increase emigration. At the same time the desire for a better standard of living for which emigration seemed the only solution, undoubtedly encouraged the postponement of marriage by the intending emigrant.

HOUSING AND SOCIAL AMENITIES

This was a period of considerable housing shortage and a relatively high degree of overcrowding. With a population which had remained static for more than 30 years, and which in the previous half century had shown a heavy decline, it might have been expected that the housing situation would have shown a steady improvement. However, there were a number of reasons why this did not happen. First, the depopulation of the land contributed hardly at all to an easier housing situation. For the most part it meant simply that fewer members of families lived in the existing houses. Irish emigration has predominantly been an emigration of individuals rather than of whole families. In cases where whole families did leave the country, their houses were frequently not sold and not maintained. Moreover, the growth of population in Dublin had caused a particularly acute housing shortage in that area. Overcrowding was at its worst in the county boroughs of Dublin, Cork, Limerick and Waterford. Apart from these areas of special difficulty, there was little difference in the pattern of the overcrowding problem as between other town and country areas.

The Census of 1946 provided evidence for the first time on the extent of such amenities as water supply and sanitation in Irish households. The results were not a matter for congratulation. It emerged, for example, that only one in every five of all the houses in the country had piped water; only one in twenty farm dwellings had piped water. The rest made do with wells, pumps and streams. Only one in every four farm dwellings had an indoor lavatory. It is clear that a glaring inadequacy of ordinary amenities like light, water supply and sanitation existed throughout the Irish countryside, which intensified the poor material standards and the drudgery of rural life. The discrepancy between the standards of life in the countryside and life in the towns and cities became increasingly marked and this was clearly an important influence in causing people to leave the land.

However, this period saw progressive improvement in the provision of housing, the elimination of overcrowding and the provision of ordinary household amenities. Overcrowding is measured for Census purposes as the ratio of the population which is living with two or more persons to a room. The 1946 Census showed that this ratio declined from 22.5 per cent in 1936, to a figure of 16.8 per cent 10 years later. The post-war period especially saw a greatly intensified housing drive. The number of new houses built with state aid was 1,180 in 1947—it was 12,305 in 1951, an elevenfold increase.

Apart from housing, this was a period of considerable advance in housing amenities such as the provision of electricity, piped water supplies and indoor sanitation. There was a distinct improvement in living standards throughout this period. Housing conditions improved substantially, overcrowding declined, life expectancy increased, and the rise in the marriage rate obviously owed something to the better economic and social conditions which were achieved.

CONCLUSION

However, the unfavourable features of Irish society throughout this period were serious: a static population suffering from heavy emigration, a uniquely unfavourable marriage pattern and a steep decline in the rural population. The decline in rural population was compensated to some extent by an increase in industrial employment and in the numbers of the town population, especially in Dublin. However, the expansion of non-farm employment was inadequate to counter-balance the numbers leaving agriculture. Emigration therefore took place in the context of a static total population and a static working population. Emigration also took its sharpest toll in the younger age groupings, which produced an ageing population and an unusually high proportion among the dependency groupings of under 15 and over 65.

The decade of the 'fifties showed little promise of producing a reversal of these socially unfavourable tendencies. Economic growth and industrial expansion were of limited proportions. The expansion of the economy was disastrously low. Emigration reached record heights and the loss of population, temporarily reversed in the post-war period, resumed again. It was not until the latter years of this decade that light began to break through at last on this gloomy and seemingly intractable scene of economic and social malaise.

Irish Foreign Policy, 1945-5

NICHOLAS MANSERGH

In October 1945 Seán Lester, the distinguished Irishman who served as the last Secretary-General of the League of Nations, noted that the first great experiment in international co-operation made by the League had ended and that its lessons should 'now contribute to the second experiment'. That second experiment was the United Nations. Its constitution was fashioned at the Dumbarton Oaks Conference in 1944, and its Charter agreed by delegates from fifty nations at San Francisco in April 1945, meeting, in the words of President Truman, as 'the architects of the better world'. Ireland was not numbered with them. Nor was she represented at the first meeting of the General Assembly on 10 January 1946, twenty-six years to the day after the creation of the League of Nations. The reason for Irish absence was neither indifference on the one side nor hostility on the other but simply that membership at the outset was confined to the allied victor powers.

An early indication of Ireland's attitude was given on 24 July 1946, when the Taoiseach, Mr de Valera, tabled a motion in the Dáil expressing Irish willingness to accept the obligations contained in the Charter and recommending that the government should take steps to secure Irish membership. In the course of the debate, Mr de Valera said that

Ireland was a peace-loving state, in agreement with the fundamental principles of the Organization and that while 'in our circumstances . . . it is impossible to be enthusiastic, I think we have a duty as a member of the world community to do our share in trying to bring about general conditions which will make for the maintenance of peace'.[1] Accordingly on 2 August the Irish government made formal application for admission but on 15 August it was successfully opposed by the Soviet Union on the ground that Ireland had no diplomatic relations with Russia.[2] For the next nine years, the Soviet Union used its veto to keep Ireland out and her admission in 1955 came at last as part of a package deal on membership between East and West. Accordingly, for the whole of the period 1946-1951, Ireland, while taking an active part in the work of some of the U.N. specialized agencies, for example, the Food and Agriculture Organization, remained none the less firmly excluded from the world's political forum. For Ireland, therefore, these were the years of waiting that preceded the years of constructive contribution.

Below the summit of world politics lay more limited but sometimes more pressing questions of regional policy. Here geography predetermined the range of Ireland's interests, though not necessarily her response. She was a part of, though not at the outset of the period a partner in, Western Europe; she lay within the area of the Atlantic Community and, through association with Britain, close to the heart of the British Commonwealth of Nations. In each capacity there was a judgement to be made, a policy to be formulated. But while the issues presented in each case were distinct and distinguishable, no Minister for External Affairs could escape the need to think out an order of preferences and priorities.

1. *Dáil Éireann, Parliamentary Debates*, cii, 1311, 1325. Mr de Valera's commentary (*ibid.*, 1308–26) on the principles and obligations of U.N. membership, based as it was on his experience of the League of Nations, is well worth reading.
   2. The probability of Russian objection was foreseen, see *Dáil Éireann, Parliamentary Debates*, cii, 1310–11.

Mr de Valera's Fianna Fáil administration and the succeeding Inter-Party government under Mr Costello were agreed on the first object of their foreign, as of their domestic, policy—namely the ending of partition. In Europe, in the Atlantic and in the Commonwealth, this had an influence upon attitudes and in two instances, at least, upon decisions taken, though in the strict sense partition in its external aspect was not a European nor an Atlantic or indeed a Commonwealth issue. It remained, as indeed it was often described, the outstanding question in Irish relations with Britain, and it assumed significance in these wider contexts only because Britain was a major power in Western Europe and in the Atlantic Community, as well as being the principal partner in the Commonwealth.

In 1945 the war in Europe ended leaving behind peoples who had 'supped full of horrors' and a continent devastated for the second time in a generation. There were two dominant preoccupations—the building up of the military strength of peace-loving peoples in the Western world so that no such disaster should happen again and the employment of every means to ensure rapid economic recovery from the devastation of war. In theory the two were distinct, but in practice by late 1947 economic recovery, indispensable on its own, had come to be thought of also, and widely, as the surest bastion against the westward march of Communism. The Irish government, however, preserved the distinction by withholding from the one and participating in the other. Ireland, accordingly, was not a signatory to the new defensive alliances in the West, from the five-power Brussels Treaty of March 1948 to the North Atlantic Treaty of April 1949, by which time the rigours of the cold war were settling in Europe and the continent was doomed to division by an iron curtain, or, as it became, by a wall dividing a city and an electrified wire barrier stretching across the fields and woodlands of its historic heartland. Successive Irish governments made no secret of their views. They were anti-Communist and pro-Western. 'Our sympathies', observed Seán MacBride, Minister for External Affairs, on 20 July 1948, 'lie clearly with Western Europe'. But he added, 'the continuance of partition precludes us from taking our rightful place in the affairs of Europe'.[3] The Irish government defined its position in the same terms but more formally in a memorandum[4] in response to an invitation to adhere to the North Atlantic Treaty Organization, in 1949. They stated that while in agreement with the general aims of the treaty, Ireland was unable to accede to it because of the occupation of the six north-eastern counties by British forces. So long as partition lasted, any alliance with Great Britain, the note continued, would expose the Irish government to the risk of civil conflict within its own jurisdiction. The most realistic approach to North Atlantic security, so far as Ireland was concerned, lay, therefore, in ending a situation which ' threatened the peace of these islands'. From that position no subsequent Irish government has departed.

No such difficulty was felt to arise in respect of Irish participation in plans for economic and social reconstruction in Western Europe, and from the outset Ireland was associated with them. The historic initiative came with General Marshall's speech on 5 June 1947 at Harvard in which he spoke of 'the dislocation of the entire fabric of the European economy', of the substantial help that must come from America and of the need for European initiatives which would allow of United States supporting action. And it was in this way that the European Recovery Programme was launched. On 12 July the Conference on European Economic Co-operation opened in Paris with Ireland represented by Mr Seán Lemass, Mr P. J. Smith, Minister for Agriculture, and Mr F. H. Boland, Secretary of the Department of External Affairs. Mr de Valera came too, for the concluding Plenary Session at which he noted that the report of the Conference recognized self-help as a primary duty, and asked

3. *Dáil Éireann, Parliamentary Debates,* cxii, 902–5.
4. Reprinted in an Exchange of Notes with the government of the United States, No. 9934.

for no more aid than was absolutely necessary if the damage
of the war years was to be made good and Europe restored.
These austere comments were no doubt welcome in the
United States where side by side with a high sense of post-
war responsibilities that inspired the Marshall Plan, 'the most
unsordid act in history', there lingered on a suspicion that in
Europe Americans were, as the phrase went, apt 'to be played
for suckers'. Subsequently Ireland, through the work of the
Organization for European Economic Co-operation, and its
reports, became accustomed to a consideration of her economic development within a European setting. The fact, however, remained that the great weight of her trading, as of
her financial interest, continued to lie not in continental
countries but with Britain. The trade agreements of 1947
and 1948, together with the strength of sterling as a currency, were fundamental; economic relations with the continent were still peripheral in their importance.

There is one other European development of these years
to be mentioned. Ireland was a founder-member of the
Council of Europe. The Council, its statute agreed in May
1950, was a purely consultative body with a committee of
ministers and an assembly, but it was also the platform for
an idea—the idea that was later embodied in the Treaty of
Rome and the Common Market. At the earlier meetings of
the Council, the Irish delegates sought to focus European
attention upon partition but later this policy was discarded
as being misconceived, and through Council membership
Ireland was drawn more closely into European thinking
about Western European union.

The most dramatic step in the years 1945-1951 was, however, taken not in respect of the North Atlantic nor of Europe
but of the Commonwealth.[5] When the war ended, the nature
of the Irish association with it was ambiguous. The British
and dominion governments for their part continued to regard
Éire as a member, taking the view that the Constitution of

5. For a more detailed account see N. Mansergh, *Survey of British Commonwealth Affairs*, 1939–1952, Oxford 1958, chapter VI.

1937 in conjunction with the External Relations Act of the preceding year had effected no fundamental alteration in Irish relations with the Commonwealth, as defined in the 1921 Treaty. Since common allegiance was at that time a conventional characteristic of dominion status, this view necessarily implied Irish allegiance in some form. The Irish government had, however, repudiated allegiance, and the Irish view, as expressed by Mr de Valera on many occasions, was that Ireland, after 1937, was a state outside the Commonwealth, associated externally with it, not owing allegiance to the Crown, and a republic in fact even though not specifically so described in the Constitution. Irish association, therefore, continued despite a divergent and conflicting interpretation of its nature, because of mutual self-interest—on the Irish side in terms of keeping open a door to national unity and on the British of preserving at least the appearance of Commonwealth unity—and on a presumably unspoken official understanding. But while it was thus the policy of governments to let sleeping dogs lie, there were others who thought it their duty to stir them up. In the Dáil, Mr Dillon enquired of the Taoiseach whether the state was a republic or not, a member of the Commonwealth or not, while at Westminster also Labour ministers were faced with Unionist questions as to whether Éire was a dominion and whether as a dominion she had been consulted, for example, about the changes in the Royal Style and Titles consequent upon the independence of India and Pakistan—to which Mr Patrick Gordon Walker replied she had been 'as a member of the Commonwealth—a Government within the Commonwealth'.[6] In such circumstances it was clearly questionable how long the ingenious but politically fragile ambiguities of the External Relations Act could continue to serve a useful purpose, and its deviser, Mr de Valera, was evidently contemplating the use of its enabling powers in other ways so as to transfer the required formalities from the Crown to the President, by a legislative enactment. The

6. *House of Commons Debates,* vol. 449, col. 1975.

results of the general election, 1948, however, predicated a more drastic solution.

The decision in principle to repeal the External Relations Act was no doubt made by the incoming Inter-Party government some time in the summer of 1948, against the domestic political background described by Professor Lyons, but the actual decision was announced by Mr Costello while on a visit to Canada. It was the timing, and not the event that was a matter for great surprise. More important, in terms of foreign policy, were the implications. There was no dispute about a dominion's right of secession and, therefore, in the British view, of Éire's right to secede. That had been explicitly conceded in 1942 when Sir Stafford Cripps, as an envoy of the British cabinet, outlined proposals for a future dominion status for India. He was asked at a press conference in New Delhi whether the new Indian dominion would have the right to disown its allegiance to the Crown. He replied that an Indian dominion 'would remain completely free to remain within or to go without the Commonwealth of Nations'. He was asked whether Canada could do so and could join the United States. He replied, 'Of course it can'.[7] But in the Irish case one point remained; did the repeal of the External Relations Act and the decision to describe the state formally as a republic necessarily imply secession from the Commonwealth? Mr Costello was asked that very question by a correspondent at a press conference in Ottawa. He replied in the affirmative. That settled what to my mind was otherwise not quite clear. I have been told, incidentally, that the correspondent who asked the question was a representative of the Russian Tass Agency. He is said to have asked it with the provisions of the Constitution of the U.S.S.R. in mind—they allowed secession in principle, though one suspects a Soviet republic which ventured to apply it in practice in Stalin's day would have needed courage. But the important thing is that Mr Costello's answer

7. The record of the press conference is in R. Coupland, *The Cripps Mission*, Oxford 1942.

in Canada was conclusive. The Irish government had decided to sever their connection with the Commonwealth.

The Republic of Ireland Bill[8] was introduced in the Dáil on 24 November 1948. The preamble stated that it was an act to repeal the External Relations Act, to declare that the description of the state should be the Republic of Ireland and to enable the President to exercise executive power or any executive function in connection with the state's external relations. This precisely describes its purpose. In introducing the Bill the Taoiseach said that when enacted it would have consequences which would mark it as a measure ending an epoch. 'This Bill will end,' he said, 'and end forever in a simple, clear and unequivocal way, this country's long and tragic association with the institution of the British Crown and will make it manifest beyond equivocation or subtlety that the national and international status of this country is that of an independent Republic'.[9] The measure was not designed or conceived in any spirit of hostility to the British people or to the institution of the British Crown; on the contrary, one result of its enactment would be that Ireland's relationship with Britain would be 'put upon a better and firmer foundation than it ever has been before'; and it would be unthinkable, Mr Costello continued, for the Republic of Ireland to draw farther away from the nations of the Commonwealth with which 'we had such long and, I think, such fruitful association in the past twenty-five or twenty-six years'.

What were reactions overseas to this dramatic step in Irish foreign policy? In Britain they were, initially, apt to be heavy with foreboding. When I was an undergraduate I remember passing an open window in College with my tutor and over-hearing from the wireless the words 'lost a bye-election at

8. No. 22 of 1948.

9. *Dáil Éireann, Parliamentary Debates,* cxiii, 347. Mr Costello's speech together with British and dominion speeches on the secession of the Republic of Ireland are reprinted in N. Mansergh, *Documents and Speeches on British Commonwealth Affairs* 1931–1952, 2 vols., Oxford 1953, vol. II, section XIV, 794–837.

Oswestry in 1904'. 'Ah,' said my tutor, 'Lord Bridgeman is dead'. To my awestruck enquiry, he replied that as a life-long Liberal he was familiar with the bye-election results of 1904 and he could not fail to remark upon the solemn obituary tones in the B.B.C. announcer's voice. It was in such tones, overlaid with more than a hint of pained reproach, that the B.B.C. on its 9 o'clock news announced Ireland's impending departure from the Commonwealth. On succeeding days there was added to the element of reproach, a dwelling upon possible consequences. There were two open questions. Did Irish citizens become aliens in Britain and in the rest of the Commonwealth? And did existing trade preferences come to an end? Each question deserves a comment.

A revolution in Commonwealth citizenship, reflected in the British Nationality Act 1948, in effect made British and Irish citizenship reciprocal. Citizens of Éire, under the provisions of this British act, would no longer be British subjects, but when in Britain they would be treated as though they were. The question after the announcement of impending Irish secession was whether the provisions of an act passed in different circumstances would continue to apply. The answer by agreement of the British and Irish governments was in the affirmative and on the basis of continued reciprocity. It was arrived at on both sides in the light of their own state interests and was generally though not universally welcomed. George Bernard Shaw for his part, and after living in England for nearly half a century, remarked—'I shall always be a foreigner here whether I have to register as an alien or not, because I am one of the few people here who thinks objectively. Englishmen are incapable of doing this.'

In respect of trade, it was suggested there was risk that the existence of preferential duties between Britain and Ireland would be challenged as conflicting with the most favoured nation clause in commercial treaties with foreign countries and with the General Agreement on Tariffs and Trade negotiated at Geneva in 1947. On this point, however, the Irish government were always, and it emerged rightly, confident. They argued that the very close and long-standing trading relations between the two countries warranted exceptional treatment and more particularly they pointed to the fact that the schedule to the Geneva Agreement listed Commonwealth countries individually by name without any general heading implying that the preferences exchanged were conditional upon Commonwealth membership. Furthermore in 1950 Ireland concluded a Treaty of Friendship, Commerce and Navigation with the United States ensuring thereby among other things that the continuance of the existing trade preferences would not be questioned in Washington.

What was the response to Irish secession in the wider Commonwealth setting? With the possible exception of the Canadian Prime Minister, Commonwealth ministers had no advance information of it. On this point the Lord Chancellor, Lord Jowitt, who made no complaint, was explicit and to Conservative critics, who maintained that Labour ministers had not done enough to persuade the Irish government to hold its hand, he replied that he was convinced that if any of them had spoken to the Irish 'with the eloquence of Demosthenes and at greater length even than Mr Gladstone he would have failed—as I failed'.[10] Irish secession was in effect settled apart from the Commonwealth. This had its importance. In Commonwealth affairs there were great changes brought about by the independence of India, Pakistan and Ceylon in 1947 and their decision to opt for membership at least provisionally. All were mother countries with their civilizations, wholly distinct from the old dominions of settlement, and India furthermore was about to become a republic. Their Prime Ministers were to attend their first Commonwealth conference in October 1948. To this conference the Irish government is understood to have been invited but it allowed the invitation to lapse. Lord Attlee commented on the detailed discussions that took place at the conference about republican membership, in recollections recorded by Francis Williams under the title *A Prime Minister Remembers*.

10. *House of Lords Debates,* vol. 159, col. 1089.

But contrary to what one might expect, there is no reference to the parallel Irish situation—which may merely serve to show how much a prime minister forgets or may possibly indicate that he had felt at the time that the two situations should be kept apart in the hope that Irish secession might in fact ease India's accession. In any case despite lack of prior consultation and the absence of Irish delegates from the meeting, the Commonwealth did play in 1948, presumably for the last time, a role—it may be thought not an unhelpful one—in Irish affairs.

That Commonwealth role had two aspects. The first was negative. The British government, it is reasonable to infer, at least considered the possibilities of a sharper reaction, presumably in respect of citizenship and trade, to Irish secession than in fact was expressed. Certainly the Lord Chancellor's speech, to which I have already referred, suggests this was so. In defending against Conservative critics, the arrangements in fact made, he urged that Britain should consider where her own advantage lay. But he also said, and it is this which deserves attention, that if the British government had taken a different line from the one they decided to take 'we should have acted in the teeth of the advice of the representatives of Canada, Australia and New Zealand'. Lawyers choose their words carefully. What lay behind this?

We know that at the time of the Commonwealth Prime Ministers' meeting in October there were separate discussions, first at Chequers and then at Paris, between representatives of the Irish government and representatives of the British, Canadian, Australian and New Zealand governments. It was at these discussions presumably that there emerged something like a united dominion view urging that Irish secession should not be allowed to impair relations between Ireland and the other countries of the Commonwealth and even, in so far as that was possible, that the way should be left open for her return—Australia's Labour Prime Minister, Mr Chiffley, later made this point with some emphasis. When Peter Fraser, New Zealand's Prime Minister, was asked what difference secession would make in New Zealand's attitude to Ireland, he replied, 'What difference could there be? There has been friendliness always', and in the New Zealand Republic of Ireland Act it was expressly stated that New Zealand law should have operation in relation to the Republic of Ireland 'as it would have had if the Republic of Ireland had remained part of His Majesty's Dominions'. In statutory terms friendship could go no further than that!

But the Republic had ceased on any reckoning to be part of His Majesty's dominions. This made a psychological difference. A well-known Australian commentator, Professor J. D. B. Miller of the Australian National University, has noted that 'the 1948 arrangements put paid to the whole score with goodwill on all sides. Except for some mild scuffling between Mr Menzies's government in Australia and the Irish government about how the Australian Ambassador to Éire should be designated later relations between Éire and the Old Dominions have little to offer the historian'.[11] More formally, Irish representatives no longer attended prime ministers' meetings. It would be interesting to speculate about the views they might have advanced in the successive crises through which the Commonwealth has passed since 1949—African membership, the Suez affair, the Common Market, South Africa's secession and Rhodesia. It is also interesting to note that by 1967 Ireland, constitutionally, would have been in a comfortable majority. There are today more republics than monarchies within the Commonwealth. It remains, indeed, one of the curiosities of recent history that in the year in which Ireland seceded, India as a Republic became a member. How does one explain the apparent paradox? I think the answer is tolerably simple. After 1916 the Republic in Ireland symbolized the cause of independence, whereas in India what mattered was the independence movement with the Republic incidental to it. This enabled the Indian government, as Pandit Nehru reminded the Indian parliament at the time, to take note of Irish External Association precedents which, as

11. J. D. B. Miller, *Britain and the Old Dominions,* London 1966, 147.

he explained, had shown Indians that it was possible to reconcile republicanism with Commonwealth membership and also to be flexible in respect of the monarch as symbolic head of the Commonwealth. To that extent others followed the path Ireland had pioneered while she elected to travel other roads. At a deeper level the Republic of India acceded to, and the Republic of Ireland seceded from, the Commonwealth because of their respective governments' interpretation of their respective state interests.

At the end it is possible to look back and see the years after the Second World War as the years in which Ireland determined the priorities of her international policies. In respect of the United Nations she was perforce limited to declaration of intent. She decided against military alliances even under the aegis of the United States—a decision seemingly less significant now than when it was made, because the supersession of conventional weapons by a still fortunately unconventional nuclear armament, including inter-continental ballistic missiles, has deprived Ireland, possibly for all time, of her former strategic importance. She also decided against continued Commonwealth membership—the most important foreign policy option made in these years and one with domestic overtones in respect of national unity. And what did it indicate? I think if one looks beyond the controversy of the time, probably it chiefly showed a sense that while Irish relations with Britain were fundamental, her relations with the Commonwealth were a superstructure and psychologically deemed more a hindrance than a help to practical co-operation. It also suggested, as Irish association with the European Recovery Programme, E.E.C. and the Council of Europe in part confirmed, a shift in interest from countries overseas where many Irish emigrants had settled to the geographical area of which Ireland is a part. Not for the first nor the last time might this be represented, with North American qualifications, as a triumph of geography over history. But here it is well to be cautious until the 'off-shore islands' of the Gaullist phraseology become a part of the European Common Market.

The Irish Party System, 1938-51

J O H N   A.   M U R P H Y

The party system finds no mention in the Constitutions of 1922 and 1937. All during our period, and for over a decade afterwards, the party affiliations of candidates could not be disclosed on ballot papers. This delicate silence on the central reality of Irish political life illustrates the difficulty of discovering the actual nature of politics from official documents. In turn, the literature of the political parties will mislead us if we expect it to tell us where power really lies in the party organizations. The Fine Gael outline of organization, for example, does not refer at all to the vital role of the front bench : there is no hint in the corresponding Fianna Fáil literature that the *ardfheis* (annual convention) is primarily a necessary piece of window-dressing and grievance-airing and that the formulation and shaping of policy is the work of a small inner circle.

The political party system of the 1920s and early 1930s continues into our period, simplified by the final disappearance of splinter groups and accentuated by the extension of party politics to new areas. Fianna Fáil had long since grasped the importance of controlling local government bodies although its main rival lagged behind here till a later period. Representation in the new *Seanad* (senate) which the 1937 Constitution piously envisaged on a functional or vocational basis, quickly

147

came to be determined along party lines. Even the high office of the Presidency was brought into the arena of party politics in 1945. After the outbreak of war in 1939 and the declaration of Irish neutrality, there were suggestions from time to time that the party system should be set aside and a national government formed. This was never done because in the last analysis Mr de Valera would not have it, secure in his comfortable majority for most of the period and confident that he and his party team could deal with the various problems presented by the war. In any case, there was never, from 1939 to 1945, a national crisis of an acute nature.

Though the party system continued to function, the war years witnessed a diminution of intensity in party politics; not until the 1948 election was there something like a return to the excitement of the 1930s. By the opening of our period the tumult of the Blueshirt days had died down, and within the parliamentary framework at least, political tempers had cooled. The passage of time was healing the great bitterness of the Civil War, albeit very slowly; the Treaty-Republic issue was ceasing to have any real meaning; and the gap between Fianna Fáil and Fine Gael political and economic policies was being narrowed. The whole tempo of political life was, of necessity, slowed down by war-time conditions. National security demanded some form of party truce which was effected in the sphere of defence. Representatives of all parties sat on the Defence Council and appeared together on recruiting platforms. The harshness of party antagonisms was also muted by the sense of national determination on the neutrality policy and by the common participation of men of conflicting political persuasions in their country's defence. Moreover, time given to the Red Cross or the local security forces meant some neglect of the affairs of the political branch. Party organization was thus impaired by 'emergency' conditions and party publicity at election times was affected by the restrictions on travel and newsprint. But the slackening in political activity was less detrimental, in the nature of things, to the party in office than to its opponents.

In June 1938, against the propitious background of the recently-concluded Anglo-Irish agreement, Fianna Fáil secured its greatest electoral triumph—52 per cent of the total vote and an overall majority of 15 seats. This greatly strengthened government was to survive for the full legal term of the Dáil. A major factor in this, as in other Fianna Fáil victories, was the remarkable efficiency of the party machine. In contrast to its principal opponent, Fianna Fáil had the advantage of being compelled, as it were, to build up a political organization from scratch in pursuit of power from the wilderness. From the late 1920s it had demonstrated a grasp of political techniques unusual at the period and an appreciation of the concept of mass organization which was never approached by its opponents. After the fashion of the old Sinn Féin clubs, the Fianna Fáil organization had been established on the basic unit of the *cumann* (association) of which there was one in almost every parish. At the other end of the scale of organization, harmony was secured at the top by ensuring that the front bench was strongly represented on the National Executive. In turn, the National Executive always kept in close touch with the *cumainn* and made sure that local viewpoints and grievances were at all times considered. Thus the party strength in the countryside was nourished, and rural distrust of Dublin headquarters held in check. The enthusiasm and energy of the voluntary worker, fired by allegiance to de Valera, was a vital ingredient of success. Full-time organizers had ceased to function as soon as the party had found its feet, and as late as 1950 an *ard-fheis* motion proposing the appointment of whole-time organizers was defeated. Headquarters fully appreciated the services of the local worker and Fianna Fáil was free from the kind of dualism which was to be a source of weakness in Clann na Poblachta and which in that party was aggravated by the condescending attitude of some progressives to the simple nationalist faith of the republican rank-and-file. Support for Fianna Fáil was of course also buttressed by the considerable patronage at its disposal—the result of long years in office, nation-wide organization and penetration of local government. Many were bound to the party by self-interest no less than by conviction.

The advanced organizational thinking of Fianna Fáil was also indicated by the establishment of its own vehicle of daily propaganda as far back as 1931 and by its successful pioneering of the annual church door collection. Though larger subscriptions from businessmen and industrialists were later forthcoming, the party organizers always impressed on the *cumainn* the psychological importance of the small subscription unit, as had the leaders of the Catholic Association in the 1820s, aware that a personal financial contribution gives a sense of involvement and identification. A further shrewd touch was the acknowledgement of even very small sums by receipts franked with the magical signature of Eamon de Valera.

The de Valera mystique continued to sustain Fianna Fáil fortunes at a later stage when disillusionment with the party was widespread. De Valera supporters then made the saving distinction between a jaded, incompetent government and a leader who, if not infallible, was certainly judged to be above corruption. His control over his cabinet and the parliamentary party was unchallenged. As a parliamentary tactician he frequently kept his own enigmatic counsel: there were occasions in the Dáil when even the party whip and the responsible minister seemed to be kept guessing until the last moment on what their leader's approach was going to be.

It was a tribute to the effectiveness of Fianna Fáil propaganda that by 1938, while still managing to give the impression of being *the* party for the underprivileged, and so retaining a wide base of support, it was at the same time becoming a party of an irreproachably respectable dye and was beginning to attract the men of property and position who had originally attached themselves to the pro-Treaty side and who had felt some dismay at the advent of de Valera to power in 1932. Fianna Fáil's industrial protectionist policy had deeply involved it with the world of business, and the pressure of businessmen in the party helped to modify its initially radical policies, as set out in its official 'aims'. In office, the party found itself using the repressive apparatus of state power in dealing with republican extremists and this also tended to change its political complexion. Another significant development was the transfer to Fianna Fáil of considerable Protestant and ex-Unionist support, already being claimed by some Fianna Fáil deputies after the 1938 election. The religious minority came to appreciate a government which was no longer militantly republican or aggressively irredentist, which was not (or at least did not seem to be) as closely identified with the Catholic middle class as its main opponents—and so not as likely to yield to Catholic clericalist pressures, real or imagined—and which above all had demonstrated its capacity to govern, dealing firmly with threats from right and left. The appointment of Douglas Hyde as President, de Valera's generous attitude towards Trinity College, the explicit assurances in the Constitution on religious toleration, and the generally just treatment in practice of the minority—all these had their effect. After the Fine Gael *volte face* on the constitutional position in 1949, there remained no logical political reason why those sympathetic to a British connection should not vote Fianna Fáil rather than Fine Gael.

The declaration and subsequent direction of the neutrality policy, though backed by all parties, redounded to the credit of Fianna Fáil and was effectively exploited to party advantage in the war-time elections. The thesis was developed that only de Valera's achievements had made neutrality feasible in the first place and only his leadership would see the country safely through the war. 'Don't change horses when crossing the stream' became the Fianna Fáil slogan in the 1943 campaign : by implication, at least, the sincerity and competence of Fine Gael in respect of neutrality were being questioned. An election jingle ran : 'If you vote Fianna Fáil, the bombs won't fall.' In the economic sphere, there was reasonable satisfaction with Lemass's maintenance of supplies : it was a profitable piece of psychology to prepare the public for the worst when the worst never came. Finally, it also benefited the government that the various exigencies of the 'emergency' period necessarily limited

F

the activities of the opposition : indeed, opposition beyond a certain limit could always be branded as a danger to national solidarity and security.

The period under review was, for the most part, a disastrous one for Fine Gael. Its association with the quasi-fascist Blueshirt movement had badly damaged its prestige and had been a traumatic experience for what was basically the most orthodox of parliamentary parties. The failure to restore its lost fortunes in the 1937 election was significant : the reasonably favourable atmosphere then prevailing, after five years of controversial Fianna Fáil rule, was destined not to be repeated. De Valera's successful negotiation of the 1938 Anglo-Irish agreement was a bad blow to Fine Gael. From then on, all the cards were stacked against the party and, after its calamitous loss of 13 seats in the 1943 election (Clann na Talmhan being the principal beneficiary), it seemed to be gloomily reconciled to a bleak future as a minority party and to lose the will to power. In 1948 its share of the vote fell below 20 per cent and it might well have been extinguished at the next election had it not been for the new lease of life given it by the formation of the coalition government.

The party never had anything like the organizational strength of Fianna Fáil, especially at the local level. It depended largely on influential individuals in the larger centres of population, and, at election times, on *ad hoc* committees of supporters. This was all right when Cumann na nGaedheal was in government, but was utterly inadequate when, as an opposition party, it needed to attract young voters and voluntary workers. It also failed to devise an effective method of fund-raising till the late 1940s. Its lack of realism was further shown by its failure to carry the party banner aggressively into local politics and by its genteel reluctance to emulate the vigorous and effective electioneering methods of its opponents. Curiously, its aloofness in this respect was in contrast with its campaigning in the 1927-32 period when it had made widespread use of advertisements in the provincial press and had displayed imagination and ingenuity in its cartoon propaganda.

Because the organization was weak and the finances low, the party tended to select as candidates well-off farmers, professional and business men. Thus there were too many amateur part-time politicians, a fact which served to perpetuate the poor state of the organization. The educational background of Fine Gael deputies was higher than that of deputies in other parties, but this was not necessarily a political asset or an adequate compensation for the absence of the full-time politician whose energy and enthusiasm meant so much to Fianna Fáil. The aura of middle-class respectability which clung to Fine Gael especially in the country towns militated against popular support at a period when, ironically, it was already losing middle-class votes to Fianna Fáil. Particularly damaging to the party in a period of revived nationalist sentiment was the imputation of 'West British' leanings.

The outbreak of the war raised a serious dilemma for Fine Gael. It realized that to support neutrality was virtually to abandon its Commonwealth position and to lose its remaining distinguishing mark, while to oppose neutrality would have been both futile and highly unpopular. In the event, it did support the national policy faithfully, even to the extent of expelling its deputy leader, James Dillon, in 1942 for his public repudiation of neutrality. Yet some suspicion persisted about the party's real feelings, and this was hardly allayed by Richard Mulcahy's advocacy in 1944 of an Anglo-Irish military alliance as a future plank in the party's platform.

Another setback was the retirement of W. T. Cosgrave from the Fine Gael leadership in January 1944. Like some of his colleagues, he seemed to regard the party's historical task as having been already accomplished in the 1922-32 period. After the 1943 debacle, Cosgrave, tired and unwell, regarded Fine Gael's future as problematical and felt that his leadership could help it no further. With his departure from the front bench there died the interest of those who had remained in active politics only out of affection and respect for Cosgrave.

It added to the impression of the party's weakness that its new leader, Richard Mulcahy, was at that time without a seat in the Dáil.

The outlook after the 1943 election seemed promising for the Labour Party which had increased its Dáil strength from 9 to 17, benefiting, particularly in Dublin, from the public reaction to the pinch of the war-time economy, the discontent with rationing, higher prices, static wages, industrial unemployment and increased emigration.

The polarization of Irish politics around the Treaty and associated issues had always relegated the Labour Party to the background. In the absence of an Irish industrial proletariat, the backbone of its support was the rural working class. Yet its natural voters, both rural and urban, had been lured away by Fianna Fáil which in the early 1930s, with its radical appeal and programme of social reform, claimed to be the true Labour Party. Labour's appeal was purely working-class : it never tried to attract a wider social support, as its English counterpart was doing with such effect. The point has been made that under a straight vote system Labour would have been compelled to diversify its membership or perish. Under P.R., however, it could continue to elect a small number of candidates with its own votes.

The party was identified in the public mind entirely with the poorer classes and thus suffered the consequences of Irish rural and small-town petty snobbery. Few professional men, even if they had been actively wooed by the party, would have cared to join Labour. The farmer was not attracted by a party which commanded the allegiance of his labouring men. If the party had unequivocally adopted Connolly's robust socialism, it might conceivably have won more industrial and urban support, as well as that of intellectuals. On the other hand, in the repressive climate of the period, socialism was a taboo concept and politically dangerous to expound. Even as it was, this timidly reformist party was periodically charged with harbouring Communist elements. One popular rural deputy always took the precaution of getting his parish priest to sign his nomination papers! It has been well said that to belong to the Labour Party in the 'thirties and 'forties was neither safe nor respectable.

Labour Party membership was almost entirely trade unionist and the parliamentary party gave the impression of a group whose main purpose seemed to be the defence of trade union interests in the Dáil. Yet despite this uncomfortably close relationship between political and industrial labour, it was painfully obvious that the general body of trade unionists did not give their allegiance to the party.

In the rural areas there was little sense of a national party with declared general objectives: rural Labour was rather a series of electoral committees, each deputy being the leader of his own party, as it were, respected by his constituents for his public service and his apparent skill in redressing their grievances.

The leadership of Labour was competent but uninspired. William Norton's talents were administrative and organizational, and he had put them to good effect in building up his own Post Office Workers' Union. In *his* view of the Labour Party there was no place for the messianic vision of the 'workers' republic'—a phrase dropped from the party policy at the behest of the Catholic hierarchy.

The favourable indications for Labour in 1943 were suddenly reversed by the party crisis of February 1944 with its background of inter-union hostility, personal antagonisms and accusations of Communist infiltration. The setting up of the new breakaway group, the National Labour Party, prevented Labour from consolidating its 1943 gains and from making a sporting bid for power in the more flexible post-war political atmosphere. More immediately, in the 1944 election, the split cost the movement a total loss of five seats. The participation of both Labour groups in the 1948 coalition paved the way for eventual reunion in 1950.

The 1943 election also witnessed the impressive début of

Clann na Talmhan ('The Children of the Land'). This new farmers' party, founded in August 1938, came to be concentrated among the small farmers of the west. It was confronted by the classic problems facing Irish political farming organizations—the difficulty of accommodating the diverse interests of farmers engaged in different types and scales of farming; the lack of cohesion between different regions; above all, perhaps, the blurring of political lines resulting from the presence of farmers in other parties with agricultural policies of their own. Nevertheless, Clann na Talmhan flourished in the early war years, drawing sustenance from farming discontent with the static agricultural prices of the 'emergency' economy. The party overcame the difficulties of war-time campaigning to win 14 seats in the 1943 election. Its performance in the Dáil, first under Michael Donnellan, and later under Joseph Blowick, was never impressive. The professed contempt of the Clann na Talmhan deputies for parliamentary politics, and their refusal to adopt the role of politicians, only reflected their political naïveté and readily exposed them to Fianna Fáil strategy. Their Dáil strength declined steadily in 1944, 1948 and 1951: the support extended to the remaining deputies was personal rather than political. The history of Clann na Talmhan once again showed that, even at a time when the economy was predominantly agricultural, a party concerned with promoting exclusively agricultural policies could not hope to win sustained substantial support from the rural community itself, let alone the electorate at large.

We may mention here two movements which failed to gain representation in the Dáil in the two war-time elections. The now forgotten Córas na Poblachta was founded by Simon Donnelly and John Dowling in 1940 and made no impression on the electorate, failing to secure the return of any candidate in the municipal elections in Dublin in 1942 and polling disastrously in the three constituencies which it contested in the 1943 general election. Its only real significance was that it reflected the periodic discontent of activists with the futility of their methods, thereby foreshadowing the later formation of Clann na Poblachta.

In the early 1940s Ailtiri na hAiseirighe ('The Architects of Resurrection') caused a much greater stir than Córas na Poblachta. Despising liberal democracy and parliamentary politics, the movement aimed at total national and cultural regeneration and at the establishment of a corporatist state which would implement the papal social encyclicals. Though it admired Salazar's work in Portugal and was sometimes accused of anti-semitism, to describe it as fascist would be both facile and unhelpful. If some of its programme sounded fanciful and freakish, it was fired by intense national idealism and impatience with the status quo. Thus it attracted much youthful support, particularly from Irish language workers— indeed the organization itself was an off-shoot of the revival movement. It had some successes in Cork and Drogheda in the 1942 municipal elections, attracted some electoral support in 1943, but was ignominiously beaten in the seven constituencies it contested in 1944, having miscalculated probable voting trends and having underestimated the amount of organizational work needed. Dissensions over the leadership troubled the movement almost from the beginning and largely contributed to its decline.

Towards the end of the war the Fianna Fáil position looked unassailable. De Valera had restored his 1943 losses and had regained his overall majority in the second war-time election in May 1944. He had been helped by his handling of what seemed to be a renewed threat to neutrality, by the Labour split and by Cosgrave's retirement. The party strength was again demonstrated in 1945 by the victory of its candidate for the Presidency, Seán T. O'Kelly, over his opponents, Seán MacEoin (Fine Gael) and Patrick MacCartan, an Independent candidate of republican background. However, MacCartan's impressive showing, particularly in Dublin, indicated that there was an increasing anti-Fianna Fáil vote not prepared to help revive the moribund Fine Gael Party.

Despite the seeming permanence of the government, dissatisfaction was growing with Fianna Fáil in 1946 and 1947. Impatience with the party's long tenure of office was combined with damaging, if eventually unfounded, rumours of corruption. A characteristic post-war desire for change manifested itself. The government was blamed when there was no immediate economic improvement at the end of the war. There was dissatisfaction with the low level of the social services, with unemployment and emigration and particularly with increased prices. In the matter of wages and prices generally, it was felt that the government was completely out of touch. A lengthy strike by national school teachers in 1946 was a significant expression of the prevailing mood of discontent (teachers were heavily represented in the new Clann na Poblachta Party). Within Fianna Fáil itself there was frustration among the younger members, as the old I.R.A. guard continued to dominate the organization.

It is against this background that we must consider the most interesting political phenomenon of the period—the sudden rise and fall of Clann na Poblachta ('Children of the Republic'). Its wellspring was the 'republican university'—the jails and internment camps of the early 1940s—and its first beginnings were the committees formed to help republican prisoners. It was formally established in Dublin on 6 July 1946 and its programme had an appeal similar to that of Fianna Fáil in 1932—an attractive blend of radical republicanism and of social and economic reform. Clann must not be considered as an entirely new party starting from scratch, since it had a ready-made core of support in those who had been republican activists in the 1930s and 1940s, and it had the blessing of many veterans of the 1916-23 period. (However, we may note the coolness of Cork republicans towards the new party in contrast with the enthusiasm of their Dublin counterparts.) The party also had a colourful leader in Seán MacBride, whose family background and whose own career—particularly his valuable legal work for republican prisoners—made him an almost automatic choice. The impression of a certain exotic element in his personality was an additional attraction in an Irish political chief. The party itself was organized on the conventional lines of the existing parties—but two differences may be noted: local election committees had a dangerous freedom in the selection of candidates, and the party leader did not hold any post within the organization, a fact which seemed to exalt him above democratic procedures and so give him a faintly authoritarian tinge.

There was considerable appeal in the party's plea for an end to the residual bitterness of the Civil War and of the 1930s. Its members were welcomed irrespective of their past affiliations—'we don't care what colour shirt you wore'. Paradoxically, then, a movement whose initial impetus was republican attracted people with a pro-Treaty or even a Blueshirt past, as well as Fianna Fáil dissidents. The prospect it held out of efficient, perhaps dynamic, government drew the attention of some young businessmen who were ready to welcome a progressive alternative to Fianna Fáil. The wide political and social spectrum of support was, under stress, to disclose a dangerous divergence of view on the relative importance of nationalist-political issues on the one hand, and socio-economic objectives on the other.

Throughout 1947 the new party developed rather too rapidly. Only Fianna Fáil had succeeded in the formidable task of building up its organization in every constituency as Clann na Poblachta now tried to do. The party's trial of strength came before it had time to establish any real cohesion or discipline, but then the timing of the challenge was not of its own choosing. Its success in two of three bye-elections in November 1947 caused de Valera to decide on an immediate dissolution before the new party could strengthen its position: indeed, he had announced before the polls that defeat for the government in any of the three constituencies would mean a general election. Clann won in Dublin County and South Tipperary and relegated Fine Gael to third place in Waterford.

The ensuing election of February 1948 was the most exciting since those of 1932 and 1933. The challenge to the government from the young party caught the imagination of the electors at home, and of outside observers, and *Life* magazine featured Seán MacBride as Ireland's 'Man of Destiny'. With a panel of 93, Clann had the second largest group of candidates. Though the number has since been criticized as far too large, the mood of the country in 1947, and the results of the bye-elections, seemed convincing proof at the time that the party was riding on the crest of a wave. Yet the nomination of so many candidates, at least two to every constituency, imposed a severe organizational and financial strain on the resources of the fledgling party. Nominating more than one candidate in a constituency is profitable only if the candidates are known to be reasonably good, and if there is a reservoir of party loyalty in the area. Yet even those Clann leaders who admitted misgivings on this score still hoped for a return of at least 20 to 25 candidates, while more starry-eyed supporters spoke about a repeat of the 1918 landslide.

From Clann's viewpoint it was a tantalizing campaign. The enthusiastic meetings, the processions and bonfires and the acclaim for the party leader recalled the colourful elections of the 1930s. But in the last ten days before polling the leader of the party sensed that the tide had turned and that feelings of doubt and caution would, after all, prevent the electors from deserting their traditional party allegiances. Clann's attitude to partition, to external relations and to the repatriation of sterling assets—as inexpertly expounded from Clann platforms—were quickly seized on by the party's opponents to discredit it in the electorate's eyes as immature and irresponsible, if not atheistic and Communistic as well!

In the event, ten candidates were returned, six from the Dublin area. The party was unlucky not to have won some extra seats, and in a number of cases the margin of defeat was exasperatingly small. (On a theoretical basis of proportionality —seats in proportion to vote percentage—its not inconsiderable poll of 173,000 votes, 13 per cent of the total, would have rewarded it with 19 seats.) The failure of Clann candidates to secure an adequate number of second preferences was crucial. It could be claimed, of course, that for a young party to win ten seats at its first attempt was a distinct victory : in fact, set against Clann's great expectations, the results were a blow to many of its followers. The comparatively poor performance of a party which had promised so well had one important psychological effect : it helped to confirm the conservatism of the electorate and militated against the prospects of other new parties which might be formed in the future.

Clann na Poblachta's decision to participate in the coalition government of 1948 was reached by a very narrow majority at a crucial meeting of the party's National Executive. Even after this, as late as the morning of the day on which the Dáil assembled, three Clann deputies were still reluctant to vote for a Fine Gael Taoiseach—even the compromise choice of John A. Costello—or to participate in a Fine Gael-led government, but loyalty to their own leader ultimately prevailed. The party decision, however, alienated the republican rank-and-file and was interpreted by many erstwhile supporters as evidence of an indecent anxiety for office on the part of Clann's leaders. Some political commentators would say that the decision to participate, to accept ministries, to limit its freedom of action, was a fatal one for the party. Yet it was inherent in the logic of the situation then obtaining. The catch-cry of the election campaign had been 'put them out' and it was now in Clann's power to drive from office an administration whose treatment of republicans made it more odious, in the eyes of Clann na Poblachta, than Fine Gael, whose anti-republican misdeeds lay, after all, in the remoter past. It may be noted also that Seán MacBride had frequently advocated the Swiss system of 'representative government'—the representation of each party in government in proportion to its parliamentary strength.

If the party had acquitted itself well in office from 1948 to 1951, it is reasonable to assume that it would have strengthened its position thereafter, not, admittedly, with the now largely alienated republican element, but with a wider cross-section of the electorate. Unfortunately, though Clann could claim credit for much of the work of the 1948-51 government, its participation in the coalition revealed the structural weakness of the party, its immaturity and lack of discipline, and the rivalry and jealousy among its leading members. Seán MacBride, as Minister for External Affairs at a busy period in the growth of new international organizations, had to travel abroad frequently. Not only did his opponents present this in a damaging light—as so much irresponsible junketing—but he himself tended to lose touch and to suffer a corresponding decline in popularity with the party. Even before the crisis of 1951, the weaknesses in Clann na Poblachta were apparent. But it was the controversy over the 'mother-and-child' scheme of Dr Noel Browne which threw the party into final disarray. Its supporters were dismayed at the bitter personal clash of its two representatives in the government, and at the apparent alignment of the leader and other prominent members of an allegedly radical party with clericalist and conservative interests. The 1951 election returns saw a drop in Clann's share of the popular vote from 13 per cent to 4 per cent and a reduction of its Dáil seats from ten to two. This was the virtual end of the party as a political force, though it continued to have a minimum existence and was not formally dissolved until September 1965. It could hardly have derived any consolation from the ironic fact that by helping to make the coalition a reality in 1948 it had contributed to the near-miracle of Fine Gael rehabilitation.

Whatever be the judgement on the coalition government of 1948-51, whether it be regarded as the product of an inglorious scramble for power between highly disparate elements or as a worthwhile experiment in party co-operation, its historical importance in the story of our party system cannot be denied. It showed that the polarization of Irish political life around the Treaty issue was not an immutable fact. Party identity and even independence had been maintained in the coalition government even to the extent of diminishing the

Taoiseach's prerogatives and collective cabinet responsibility, yet men of conflicting political backgrounds *had* worked together for over three years. Electorally, this political experiment resulted in a new phenomenon—the appearance of a coalition outlook among the voters. In the 1951 election, solid coalition voting was very evident in the distribution of preferences and it was clear that the electorate now recognized a new, even if temporary, choice—Fianna Fáil versus the rest. The dominant political issues were also changing : the election of 1951 had been brought about, not by a dramatic clash between Church and state but by the mundane factor of the defection of two deputies over the government's refusal to increase the price of milk. Similarly, the 1951 election campaign was concerned more with bread-and butter considerations than with nationalist-political issues or the implications of the Browne controversy.

The coalition period had left its mark on the three main parties. The spell in opposition was a salutary corrective to Fianna Fáil complacency and gave it the incentive to overhaul the party organization, a process in which Mr Seán Lemass took a leading part. At the same time, the weakness of the coalition government confirmed Fianna Fáil in its conviction that it alone was competent to rule. Fine Gael had got its first taste of office for sixteen years and regained its self-confidence. It turned to the business of organizing itself properly and of interesting youth in the party. A gain of nine seats in 1951 reflected its improved political fortunes, and with a respectable representation of forty, it could face the future with confidence. Labour, too, by its membership of the coalition had gained in experience and responsibility and had restored its unity. Yet the coalition period had resulted in comparatively little legislation of specific benefit to Labour, William Norton's main preoccupation being with the maintenance of inter-party co-operation and the continuing existence of the government as a whole.

The effect of the electoral system on the fortunes of the

political parties within our period may be briefly commented on here. It is generally admitted that the tendency of proportional representation to make for a multiplicity of parties (and, arguably, for unstable government) was modified in the Irish context by two factors—first, the continuation of pro- and anti-treaty politics which concentrated the great majority of the electorate in two camps : secondly, the abolition, in the constituency revisions of 1935 and 1947, of the nine-, eight- and seven-seat constituencies with a huge increase in the number of three-seat constituencies, a process which favoured the larger parties and diminished the prospects of the smaller and the new parties, though these continued to be more advantageously placed than they would have been under a majority system. They did relatively well where a limited number of candidates contested elections in constituencies where reasonable support could be expected and when second preferences were forthcoming. We have already remarked the poor return of seats secured by Clann na Poblachta in 1948 in proportion to the percentage vote polled : it is interesting to note, in this connection, that Clann na Talmhan (44 candidates), with only 11 per cent of the poll in 1943, got fourteen seats. Though the Fianna Fáil Party was able to overcome the difficulties of P.R. and secure overall majorities when circumstances were particularly favourable (as in 1938 and 1944), de Valera realized at an early stage the problem of getting single-party majorities and full-length parliamentary terms under the existing system, and from 1938 was consistent in his opposition to it.

With the decrease in the number of multiple-seat constituencies in the 1935 and 1947 revisions, it might be expected that the chances of Dáil representation for Independent deputies would be considerably lessened. But the potentialities of P.R. continued to be realized for Independents. The individual who stood outside the parties (or who wore a party label lightly) had still a part to play on the Irish political stage where personal and local considerations were most important. Thus the active and well-connected local man, already prominent in local government, and perhaps with a national record or an athletic background, was always welcomed by the electorate particularly if he had the reputation of working hard to forward the interests of his constituents. In the Dáil the Independent deputies had a recognized status and were treated as a group for procedural purposes. From 1932 to 1948 de Valera did not have to depend on their support: indeed, with some exceptions, it would not have been forthcoming, for, as a group, they disliked and feared his power. When the coalition was formed in 1948, the support of some of the twelve Independents was vital: those of them willing to adhere to a coalition were consulted and the important Ministry of Agriculture given to the most prominent of their number, James Dillon. After the 1951 election it was with the support of Independents that de Valera returned to power.

Various criticisms of the party system throughout our period could be all too easily made. They might include the rigidity of party discipline in the Dáil; the importuning of government departments by deputies on behalf of their constituents; and the excessive importance attached to family connections, national records and sporting achievements, resulting in the selection of mediocre candidates. Yet, despite its recurring moods of disillusion, the Irish electorate of our period clearly chose to continue the party system and rejected proposals for an all-party government as well as the occasional right-wing suggestions of government on a corporate or on a vocational basis. Perhaps mediocrity is an unavoidable feature of parliamentary representation and part of the price to pay for maintaining parliamentary democracy. We might console ourselves with the words of Edmund Burke, penned in a far different political atmosphere and with very different political parties in mind, but no less applicable to the Irish scene from 1938 to 1951. 'Party divisions,' said Burke, 'whether on the whole operating for good or evil, are things inseparable from free government. This is a truth which, I believe, admits little dispute, having been established by the uniform experience of all ages.'

SOURCES AND SELECT BIBLIOGRAPHY

Information conveyed to writer from members of various parties.

Daily newspapers for the period.

$\begin{cases} \textit{Córas Bua} & \text{Fianna Fáil party literature.} \\ \textit{Bealach Bua} & \end{cases}$

Scheme of Organization: Fine Gael party literature.

Official election returns from 1944.

The Leader.

J. L. McCracken, *Representative Government in Ireland,* 1919–1948, London 1958.

Cornelius O'Leary, *The Irish Republic and Its Experiment with Proportional Representation,* Notre Dame University Press, Indiana 1961.

James Hogan, *Election and Representation,* Cork 1945.

J. F. S. Ross, *The Irish Election System,* London 1959.

Basil Chubb, *The Government: An Introduction to the Cabinet System in Ireland,* Dublin 1961.

T. P. Coogan, *Ireland Since the Rising,* London 1966.

Michael McInerney, 'Dr Noel Browne: A Political Portrait', *Irish Times,* 9–16 October 1967.

Michael McInerney, 'Mr John A. Costello Remembers', *Irish Times,* 4–8 Sept. (especially 7 Sept.) 1967.

Literature and Society, 1938-51

AUGUSTINE MARTIN

Our period opens with 1938, a year of culminations and beginnings in Irish writing. The first edition of *Finnegans Wake* was with the printers—though it had been completed six years before—and would appear in the following year. Yeats's last, and perhaps most perfect play, *Purgatory*, was produced at the Abbey Theatre. It was the year in which Austin Clarke's *Night and Morning* was published, a book which launched him on his finest period of poetic creation; it was the year in which Samuel Beckett published his first novel, *Murphy*. Seán O'Faolain was working on his third and last novel, *Come Back to Erin*. The third volume of Francis MacManus's trilogy, *Men Withering,* and Daniel Corkery's last volume of stories, *Earth out of Earth*, were to appear in the following year. Austin Clarke had finished the second of his three medieval prose romances, and Seán O'Casey was putting the finishing touches on the first volume of his autobiographies, *I Knock on the Door*. It was also the year in which James Stephens from his London exile brought out his last volume of poetry, *Kings and the Moon*. Kate O'Brien's *Pray for the Wanderer* and Elizabeth Bowen's *Death of the Heart* came out in that year; Liam O'Flaherty's most distinguished historical novel, *Famine*, was in the hands of the reviewers.

167

In 1939 Yeats died having given his celebrated and difficult charge to the living generation :

> . . .Irish poets learn your trade
> Sing whatever is well made,
> Scorn the kind now growing up
> All out of shape from toe to top,
> Their unremembering hearts and heads
> Base-born products of base beds. . .[1]

The generation of writers he addressed did not find it an easy assignment in a world that was beginning to appear peculiarly out of joint and a society which provided small accommodation for the poet's ministry. There were still writers like Padraic Colum, Daniel Corkery and Robert Farren who could deal with Irish material in terms of ' traditional sanctity and loveliness', but the dominant literary mood was far from celebratory. Looking back at that moment Micheál Mac-Liammóir wondered,

> What was to come to Ireland now . . . striving to visualize the future of the arts in this rain-sodden country, turning restlessly from side to side in her long, dream-haunted sleep? Would the new era born of the turmoil of 1916 replace the creative energy of his (Yeats's) labour? What new stamp would be pressed into the changing wax, softening again into shapelessness with the death of the poet? [2]

The unease and shapelessness which Mr MacLiammóir discerned in the Irish literary consciousness at this period sprang from many sources. Yeats's death at once underlined and aggravated them. He had been the great link with the Irish

1. *Collected Poems*, London 1956.
2. *All for Hecuba*, revised ed. Dublin 1961 (1st ed. London 1946).

literary revival of the previous century; he had shown younger writers like Austin Clarke, Padraic Colum, F. R. Higgins and Robert Farren the relevance of the past and the importance of a living tradition. His stance had been aloof and aristocratic but it had guaranteed the dignity if not the pertinence of the writer's trade in his country's life. With his death the tradition which he had founded and nurtured had to make its way alone.

But in a sense it had been easier for Yeats; his aloofness had insulated him from both the assault and the indifference of society; a society which was still stunned and unsettled by a revolution and a civil war; which was predominantly Catholic, middle-class and conservative; which wished to exclude from its ethos those elements that were associated with the Protestant ruling class of the pre-revolutionary period. One of these elements happened to be literature, especially such literature as challenged or criticized the new orthodoxy. Seen in the perspective of social history this philistinism is perhaps understandable; but it was a considerable source of irritation and bitterness to the Irish writer of the time. For more than a decade the Irish Censorship Board, by banning the works of writers like Liam O'Flaherty, Frank O'Connor, Seán O'Faolain and Austin Clarke, had served to alienate the Irish writer from his people. This was bad for society because it became increasingly cut off from the criticism of its most sensitive commentators; bad for the writers because their vision tended to grow sour, their attitude to society more mordant and aggressive.

It is important, on the other hand, not to see the Irish writer's alienation from his society as a purely local phenomenon. A similar sense of disillusion and alienation is to be found in the work of contemporary American writers like John Dos Passos, James T. Farrell, Thomas Wolfe and John Steinbeck; and in Britain the work of Auden, Spender, Mac-Neice and Orwell, to mention but a few, was eloquent of bitterness and disaffection. It was a time when the artist was uneasy not only about his place in society but even about his place in the cosmos; and this sense of uncertainty found one of its most eloquent manifestations in the figure of Beckett's *Murphy,* that 'seedy solipsist' strapped naked to his rocking-chair in London exile, his mind 'a large hollow sphere, hermetically closed to the universe without'.

But while English and American writers belonged to a society massive and dense enough to take the charge of their hostility without giving way, the Irish writer's world was, as yet, largely insubstantial and inchoate. Indeed the only institution which had genuine density and coherence was the Catholic Church, and it is against it that a great deal of the satirical writing of the 'thirties and 'forties is directed. It might indeed be argued that the anti-clericalism of Irish writing during this period differs from continental anti-clericalism in that it is altogether social in its slant and intention. It is hardly ever accompanied by genuine atheism; it is only very rarely anti-Christian; it is rather a function of the writer's impatience with a society within which the clergy are at once the most formidable, consistent and identifiable element.

Whatever the motivation, it is clear that social criticism in Irish literature during these two decades is largely inseparable from the question of clericalism. Liam O'Flaherty had struck the first major chord in 1929 when he published his hilariously scurrilous 'travel book', *A Tourist's Guide to Ireland.* Seán O'Faolain satirized clerical autocracy and puritanism with devastating finesse in such a story as 'The Man who Invented Sin'. Frank O'Connor anatomized the vice of cupidity with Chaucerian deftness in the character of Father Ring. But these are largely occasional exercises on the part of writers whose fiction was a searching but sympathetic exploration of their country's social and spiritual consciousness. A writer whose work took on the task of radical social and religious satire was the poet, Austin Clarke. In his verse plays, his prose romances, but more particularly in his poetry, he bodied out the predicament of the free spirit in a society which, to his mind, was determined to subjugate it. In a fighting quatrain like this, one finds him striking at both censors and priests:

Burn Ovid with the rest. Lovers will find
A hedge-school for themselves and learn by heart
All that the clergy banish from the mind,
When hands are joined and head bows in the dark.[3]

And in one of his most brilliant lyrics, 'The Straying Student',
he dramatizes the liberation of a young clerical student from
the disciplines of his vocation, and his discovery of imaginative
freedom through art. But the poem ends in an almost neurotic
vision of the artist in terror lest the muse betray him to a
world geared for his defeat:

Awake or in my sleep I have no peace now,
Before the ball is struck, my breath is gone,
And yet I tremble lest she may deceive me
And leave me in this land where every mother's son
Must carry his own coffin and believe,
In dread, all that the clergy teach the young.[4]

In Austin Clarke one can discern on the one hand the man
who suffered and enjoyed, and on the other hand the man who
fought back. It is in the fusion of the two that the bristling
satirist of the later poems was born.

But the most strenuous confrontation between artist and
society took place in the pages of *The Bell* under the editor-
ship of Seán O'Faolain. This magazine despite its uncom-
promising trenchancy was neither hostile nor destructive in
its intention; it attempted to provide a platform upon which
the people of Ireland might, in Mr O'Faolain's phrase, 'create
an image of themselves'.[5] It was founded in 1940 and in the
fifteen years of its existence it dealt with every urgent issue on
the Irish scene—medicine, agriculture, religion, republicanism,
civil liberties, old-age pensions, housing, unemployment, the

---

3. 'Penal Law', *Night and Morning* 1938; also included in *Later Poems*,
Dublin 1961.
4. *Night and Morning;* also included in *Collected Poems*, Dublin 1961.
5. See 'This is Your Magazine', by the Editor. *The Bell*, I/1, Oct. 1940.

press, the civil service, education, censorship, the Irish language. While its programme was wholly constructive it felt it part of its duty to destroy the disabling 'myths' to which Irish society had fallen victim—'the Gaelic Myth, and the other Myths like the Noble Peasant, and a host of susceptibilities born of History, which have a confining effect on all Irish thought'.[6]

It was a dashing and courageous magazine that met every attack head on and responded vividly to every issue that agitated the surface of Irish life. Seán O'Faolain compared himself to 'a sort of Flying Dutchman perpetually battling around the Cape of Good Hope in a grand Wagnerian storm', but he insisted valiantly—if not very humbly—'the work of every Irish Flying Dutchman consists in making sail boldly by dead reckoning in the dark, uncharted, with only two points of observation—between a faint star that calls itself the Spirit of Human Liberty and a vast fog compounded of the Humbug, Hypocrisy, Selfishness and Cowardice of our ruling snob classes'.[7] On a more hopeful—if rather plaintive note— he could write :

> Well . . . Who knows? Perhaps, down there in that once seventh city of Christendom; some day, a leader of a government may dine with a leader of the opposition, a Catholic Archbishop sup with a Protestant Provost, even a banned novelist with the censor that banned him. It is, one thinks, looking out again at the dim fabric of the capital and the low, far horizons of three counties, such a lovely country to look at, its Happy Men are such good companions, it has so much natural warmth and natural wisdom : a very little more and a very little less— shorter memories, longer rope for everybody, less peasant

6. See 'The Pleasures and Pains of Ireland', by the Editor, *The Bell*, VIII/5, Aug. 1944.
7. See 'On Editing a Magazine' by the Editor, *The Bell*, IX/2, 1944.

caution, more efficiency, more tolerance, and She could be—shall we say will be—the land we all dreamed of thirty golden years ago.[8]

How close we are to that dream in 1969 I won't venture to say; but what we owe as a nation to Seán O'Faolain and his successor, Peadar O'Donnell, for their management of *The Bell* during these crucial years is altogether immeasurable.

In purely literary terms, the achievement of *The Bell* was equally impressive. One of the endemic difficulties in the effort to establish and sustain a separate Irish tradition has always been the problem of publication. *The Bell* made it not only possible but attractive for the Irish writer to publish his work at home, for his own people. A glance at its successive editions shows how well the magazine catered for this need. Here we find Frank O'Connor's 'Bridal Night' and 'The Long Road to Ummera', Seán O'Faolain's 'The Silence of the Valley' and 'The Trout', Liam O'Flaherty's 'The Wedding' and 'The Lament'. In its pages are to be found the first chapters of Patrick Kavanagh's brilliant novel, *Tarry Flynn,* and James Plunkett's early stories, 'The Half-Crown' and 'Janey Mary'. Conor Cruise O'Brien published in it a number of the component chapters of his distinguished critical work *Maria Cross,* and there was poetry from a new generation of poets, Valentin Iremonger, John Hewitt, Roy McFadden, Thomas Kinsella and John Montague. The foundation of two other magazines, *Envoy* and *Irish Writing* towards the end of our period helped to consolidate the work of *The Bell* : in their numbers are to be found the work of established writers like Elizabeth Bowen and Samuel Beckett, side by side with the work of younger talent such as Mary Lavin, Anthony Cronin, Pearse Hutchinson, Ewart Milne and David Marcus, and a writer like Benedict Kiely whose real flowering in the novel was not to come until the next decade.

8. See 'The Pleasures and Pains of Ireland' by the Editor, *The Bell,* VIII/5, Aug. 1944.

In 1944 three young poets, Valentin Iremonger, Robert
Greacen and Bruce Williamson, published a small fighting
volume entitled *On the Barricade,* which announced a break
with inbred Irish tradition that had grown up around Yeats
and called for a more international awareness in Irish verse.
The volume and the stance were symptomatic of a decade in
which Irish poetry took several different directions. Austin
Clarke continued to write within the 'Gaelic mode', his satiric
vision finding increasingly vivid expression in the endless
experiment of his prosody. Robert Farren in his long poem on
St Colmcille, *The First Exile,* published in 1944, achieved a
fine magniloquence in his adaptation of Gaelic metre and
assonance. On the other hand Patrick Kavanagh whose long
poem *The Great Hunger* appeared first in 1942 and later in
his collection of 1947, *A Soul for Sale,* impatiently kicked over
the traces of tradition. The last stanza of his lyric, 'In Memory
of Brother Michael', reveals his posture :

> Culture is always something that was,
> Something pedants can measure,
> Skull of bard, thigh of chief,
> Depth of dried-up river.
> Shall we be thus forever?
> Shall we be thus forever? [9]

Kavanagh was determined that we should not, and in *The
Great Hunger* he embarked on a most penetrating scrutiny of
Irish rural life as exemplified in the life of his hero, Patrick
Maguire, the ageing and desolate bachelor 'who made a field
his bride' : here was a final refutation of the 'Noble Peasant'
myth :

> The cows and horses breed,
> And the potato-seed
> Gives a bud and root and rots
> In the good mother's way with her sons;

9. *A Soul for Sale,* London 1947.

The fledged bird is thrown
From the nest—on its own.
But the peasant in his little acres is tied
To a mother's womb by the wind-toughened navel-cord
Like a goat tethered to the stump of a tree—
He wanders around and around wondering why it
    should be.
No crash,
No drama
That was how his life happened.
No mad hooves galloping the sky,
But the weak, washy way of true tragedy—
A sick horse nosing around the meadow for a clean place
    to die.[10]

By the time he had come to write his remarkable novel, *Tarry Flynn* (1948), Kavanagh's vision had mellowed considerably, but his picture of life in the rural Monaghan of his childhood retains its extraordinary authenticity. It is still a poet's vision curiously compounded of lyricism and realism; in *Tarry Flynn* it has given us one of the most imperishable novels to come out of modern Ireland.

Denis Devlin's volume of 1946, *Lough Derg and Other Poems*, made comparatively little impact on the Irish reading public. Indeed since his death in 1959, despite the publication of his work in definitive editions by Brian Coffey for the Dolmen Press, his reputation stands higher outside than inside his own country.

Devlin was, of course, a difficult poet, formidably learned, strenuously and sometimes obscurely allusive, adventurous and profound in his religious thought—the one Irish poet of his generation with a full European sensibility. The first two stanzas of 'Lough Derg'—perhaps the only modern Irish poem after Yeats to which one might risk the ascription of greatness —reveal how effortlessly he could move from precise local observation to a commanding vision of Western tradition:

10. *Ibid.*

> The poor in spirit on their rosary rounds,
> The jobbers with their whiskey-angered eyes,
> The pink bank clerks, the tip-hat papal counts,
> The drab, kind women their tonsured mockery tries,
> Glad invalids on penitential feet
> Walk the Lord's majesty like their village street.
>
> With mullioned Europe shattered, this Northwest,
> Rude-sainted isle would pray it whole again:
> (Peasant Apollo! Troy is worn to rest.)
> Europe that humanized the sacred bane
> Of God's chance who yet laughed in his mind
> And balanced thief and saint: were they his kind? [11]

Publisher and editor have done justice to Denis Devlin; but he still awaits serious critical attention.

Our period was a lean one for the Irish theatre. MacLiammóir and Edwards between tours abroad continued to maintain high standards of acting and production in foreign plays, but no new Irish playwright of notable stature appeared at the Gate. Denis Johnston after his two splendid contributions of the previous decade, *The Old Lady Says No* and *The Moon on the Yellow River,* made a single successful return with *The Dreaming Dust,* 1940, and Mr MacLiammóir had two reasonable but lightweight successes with his *Where Stars Walk* and *Ill Met by Moonlight.* Lord Longford kept up a fine repertoire in classical drama, interrupting it occasionally to put on a new Irish play such as Austin Clarke's *Sister Eucharia* in 1939.

But the Abbey was having a particularly lean period: glancing through its lists one sees a repetition of the established names in unremarkable plays—slight pieces by George Shiels, Lennox Robinson, Louis D'Alton, B. G. McCarthy, Joseph Tomelty, Frank Carney. With O'Casey's comedies of the period—*Purple Dust* (1940) and *Cock-a-Doodle-Dandy*

11. *Collected Poems of Denis Devlin,* edited and with an Introduction by Brian Coffey, Dublin 1964.

unobtainable (1949)—the only creative excitement was generated by the works of young playwrights such as M. J. Molloy and Walter Macken. Neither entirely fulfilled his early promise. Molloy's two early plays, *Old Road* (1943) and *The King of Friday's Men* (1948), seemed to indicate a distinguished talent, but his later works lacked intensity. Macken reached his highest peak of dramatic achievement with *Twilight of a Warrior* (1955) and thereafter applied most of his energies to fiction.

It was left to the smaller, less organized groups to break away from the confining naturalism of the Abbey and restore poetry to its place in the theatre. In 1938 Austin Clarke, Robert Farren and Ria Mooney founded the Lyric Theatre Company and the Dublin Verse-Speaking Society which produced an excellent series of verse-drama through the following years, in the Peacock Theatre, on Radio Éireann and on Sunday nights at the Abbey. Among its most valuable achievements were Austin Clarke's *The Son of Learning, The Flame, As the Crow Flies* and *The Kiss*, and Donagh MacDonagh's lively ballad comedy, *Happy as Larry*, which went on to triumph in London's West End. During the same period the Abbey seems to have produced no verse plays other than Robert Farren's *Assembly at Druim Ceat* and *Lost Night* and Austin Clarke's *Black Fast* in 1941. But their policy—derived, in fact, from Yeats himself—of favouring 'good bad plays' rather than 'bad good plays' was ultimately unfortunate. Their standards declined so steeply that in 1947 Valentin Iremonger stood up in the stalls between the acts of an O'Casey production, made a speech against the management's policy and together with Roger McHugh and other friends walked out in protest. It was perhaps the nadir of the Abbey's achievement; happily standards rose during the 'fifties and continue to rise.

Our period was a good one for the Irish short story. While Frank O'Connor, Seán O'Faolain and Liam O'Flaherty were adding to their achievement with such collections as *Crab Apple Jelly, Teresa* and *Two Lovely Beasts*, a talented new writer had appeared in the person of Mary Lavin. Her first volume, *Tales from Bective Bridge* (1944), showed exceptional maturity, and before the decade had passed she had produced two novels, *The House in Clewe Street* and *Mary O'Grady*, as well as two further collections of short stories, *The Becker Wives* and *The Long Ago*. Her work was almost entirely free from the social tensions that have been glanced at earlier but rather concerned itself with what she herself described as 'the vagaries of the human heart'. She explored the middle-class ethos of Irish society with a blend of tranquillity and psychological penetration that made her almost unique among the writers of her period. As an artist she owed little to the Irish short story writers who had gone before her. Her master was Chekhov and even her earliest stories showed a remarkable and highly individual sense of organic form. Her finest single volume is perhaps *The Long Ago* which must surely rank as one of the most outstanding in the Irish tradition.

Michael McLaverty whose collection *The Game Cock* was published in 1947 had already established a reputation with such novels as *Call My Brother Back* and *Lost Fields*. He is probably the most purely lyrical of the Irish fictionists; his stories exhibit a remarkable sensitivity to the Ulster landscape of his childhood. Bryan MacMahon's first collection, *The Lion Tamer* (1949), revealed a lyrical talent as energetic as McLaverty's was meditative. In it he evoked the people and the landscape of Kerry with a vivid and unembarrassed romanticism. More recently he has remarked that his aim as a writer is 'to celebrate the pieties of my people'; and to this extent his work may be seen as a reaction against the more adversary social vision of his elder contemporaries.

Between the extremes of satire and celebration stand three novelists of this period, Francis Stuart, Kate O'Brien and Francis MacManus: like Mary Lavin in the short story, all three writers went about their task without notable reference to the social pressures which so exercised their contemporaries. Francis Stuart began his post-war period with a terrible and brilliant novel, *The Pillar of the Cloud* (1948), in which he catches the despair and desolation of an Irish exile in a shattered and humiliated German town, and followed it with his equally impressive *Redemption* in 1949. Similarly the decade drew from Kate O'Brien two of her most perfect novels : *The Land of Spices* (1941) which so accurately and delicately portrayed life in an Irish convent—and which had the distinction of being banned because of a single sentence— and *That Lady* (1946) her superb historical novel set in Renaissance Spain. All three novelists have suffered from undeserved critical neglect and of the three, Francis Mac-Manus has suffered most. Having brought his massive trilogy to a close in 1939, MacManus went on to write three of his best novels before the next decade was out—*Watergate* (1942), *The Greatest of These* (1943) and *Fire in the Dust* (1949). Of these, *Watergate* is at once the most modest in size and scope and the most perfect in form and quality. Its theme is land and the Irishman's lust for its possession. MacManus had taken up the theme five years before in *This House was Mine*, and now he explores it in terms of two related families rooted in the rich farmland of Kilkenny. It is a taut, economical novel in which character and plot are finely integrated; and the final chapters in which the tinker woman, Ruby Butt, and her idiot child are expelled from Watergate into the rainy dawn while Alice Lennon sits by the dying fire in her cold frenzy of guilt and triumph are among the most memorable in modern Irish fiction.

Our period begins with Beckett's *Murphy*, a book in which the absurdity of man's condition is caught in superb comic vision. It is proper that we should end our discussion with two Irish writers in whose work a sense of the absurd and the comic is developed to an exceptional degree, Flann O'Brien and Mervyn Wall. *At Swim Two Birds* is a work of hilarious complexity in which the author combines realism, fantasy, myth, satire and parody. The entire fabric of the book issues from the brain of a seedy undergraduate at University College, Dublin, whose 'spare-time literary activities' involve the writing of a book in which the characters he creates take on autono-

mous life and in turn create other characters endowed with
equal creative irresponsibility. Soon the crazy world of the
hero's mind is populated with characters as diverse as Fionn
MacCool reincarnated from Irish legend, a 'species of Irish
devil' called the Pooka MacPhellimey, a Good Fairy, a working-class poet, some cowboys and the mad medieval king,
Sweeney. This anarchic world of the imagination is under-
pinned by the realistic depiction of a group of down-at-heel
undergraduates who lead a life of comic squalor in University
College and the surrounding pubs. It might be said that while
the hermetically sealed mind of the Beckett hero broods
increasingly on nothingness, the mind of O'Brien's hero
encloses a wild, proliferating infinity. The book constitutes a
more colourful and marginally more comforting vision of
human absurdity. It has been frequently remarked that behind
At Swim Two Birds the work of Sterne, Joyce, Proust, Piran-
dello and Kafka can be discerned; to these might be added
the seminal influence of James Stephens whose blends of
realism and fantasy in *The Crock of Gold*, and more particularly *The Demi-Gods*, and whose exploration of world-within-
world in *In the Land of Youth*, were published before *Ulysses*
was written. By 1940 O'Brien had written his second and to
my mind his greatest novel, *The Third Policeman*, in which
he continues his experimentation with different planes of
reality and different concepts of time. But for reasons too
complex to deal with here the book was not published until
1967, when the author had died, and does not therefore fall
within the period under discussion.

While Flann O'Brien engages in formal social satire only in
two of his minor works—his play *Faustus Kelly* (1943) and his
brilliant fantasy in Irish, *An Béal Bocht*—Mervyn Wall adopts
it as his primary form. As Austin Clarke had done before
him in prose and verse, Mr Wall chooses medieval Ireland,
the island of saints and scholars, as the setting for his first two
novels, *The Unfortunate Fursey* (1946) and *The Return of
Fursey* (1948). His hero is a little monk whose intractable
innocence makes it quite impossible for him to live in the

devious society to which he is consigned. When demons infest his monastery at Clonmacnoise he is their solitary victim, because his stammer prevents him from pronouncing the words of exorcism. He becomes a reluctant outcast, his only friend the devil—and it is wholly consonant with the author's vision of society that Satan is by far the most attractive character in that medieval landscape.

The relevance of the fable to modern Ireland did not need to be underlined, as we see for instance in that passage which describes the descent of the censor on the monastery library :

> ... He was an active and conscientious man, and in each monastery which he had visited he had left behind him a heap of cinders where there had been previously treasured manuscripts of secular and pagan origin. He had been only three weeks at Clonmacnoise, but already he had committed to the flames most of the Greek and Latin manuscripts, as well as four copies of the Old Testament, which he had denounced as being in general tendency indecent. He was a small, dark man with a sub-human cast of countenance. One of his principal qualifications for the post of Censor was that each of his eyes moved independently of the other, a quality most useful in the detection of hidden meanings. Sometimes one eye would stop at a word which might reasonably be suspected of being improper, while the other eye would read on through the whole paragraph before stopping and travelling backwards along the way it had come, until the battery of both eyes was brought to bear on the suspect word. Few words, unless their consciences were absolutely clear, could stand up to such scrutiny; and the end of it usually was that the whole volume went into the fire. When he had first arrived at Clonmacnoise he had explained his method to the heart-broken librarian.
>
> 'I've an old mother,' he said, 'who lives in a cottage on the slopes of the Macgillicuddy Reeks. She is for me the type of the decent, clean-minded people of Ireland. I use

her as a touchstone. Whenever I'm in doubt about a
word or phrase, I ask myself would such word or phrase
be used by her.'

The librarian mildly enquires whether the old woman can
read. ' "No," replied the Censor indignantly, "she's illiterate.
But I don't see what difference that makes." ' [12]
The two Fursey books are remarkable examples of the
satiric stance, the comic vision. The world created in them
is altogether consistent, sustained by its own crazy laws; yet
the double vision of the satire never falters: it never ceases
to be medieval Ireland—'where anything can happen to anyone, at any time, in any place; and it usually does'—and it
never ceases to be Ireland of the 'forties at which the author's
fire is of course chiefly directed.

Mervyn Wall's most powerful novel, however, was *Leaves
for the Burning,* which was published in 1952 but which
explores Irish society during the period under discussion. It is
in a sense a divided book; its idiom is that of social realism
but its tone and vision are radically satirical. Its hero is Lucian
Burke, an educated and sensitive man trapped in a provincial
town as a junior government clerk. He is bitter and dis-
appointed, personally conscious of his personal failure, and of
Ireland's failure to found an honest and civilized society. His
days are spent in pointless clerical work, his evenings in drink-
ing with such characters as the trogloditic Dr F. X. Thullabawn and the alcoholic local engineer, Bob McMunn. The
action of the book concerns an extended binge in which the
three travel in a car through the Irish midlands in the
company of Lucian's university friend, Frank Peebles, a failed
and disillusioned artist.

The precise and realistic detail of their squalid adventure
accumulates into an indictment of a society which has failed;
in which a political revolution has resulted in the triumph of
Yeats's 'Paudeens'—in back-door politics, pious opportunism,

12. M. Wall, *The Return of Fursey,* London 1948, 82–3.

philistinism and the despair of the sensitive. The events of the
novel take place in the year of Yeats's re-internment, and
Peebles, as he announces in a post-card to Lucian, is proceed-
ing to the funeral 'on foot, through sheer eccentricity'. When
Lucian introduces him to Thullabawn, the doctor responds
with the words, 'Sorry to hear of your trouble. . . Was he a
relative or just a friend?' And the presence of Yeats broods
over the action as an elegiac and reproachful counterpoint to
their joyless dissipations.

The details of these adventures are chosen carefully to
register a sense of the absurd not altogether alien from what
Beckett and O'Brien achieved with less realistic conventions.
A grotesque creature called Lorcan O'Friel, who claims to
have lost an eye in the War of Independence, pursues the four
revellers in a relentless search for political patronage. In
drunken exasperation, the occupants of a lounge bar throw
him out of the window. It is only when his corpse is discovered
on the gravel below that they remember that the lounge in
which they have been roistering is on the first floor. Towards
the end of the book Frank Peebles attempts suicide and fails
in this as in everything he had attempted. When Lucian
returns to his office at the end of the book he is wounded in
a successful attempt to protect the petty cash box—containing
one shilling and eightpence—from a gunman in a secret
political organization. Indeed the book attempts through an
almost completely successful fusion of realism and satire to
register a vision of society in which

> The best lack all conviction while the worst
> Are full of passionate intensity.

As an adversary portrait of Irish provincial life in the late
'thirties there is nothing in our fiction to match it.

It would be too simple to call *Leaves for the Burning* a
particularly typical Irish novel of the period, because the times
were too confused and contradictory to be rendered in any
single vision. It was a time when the dirge was frequently

G

drowned by the manifesto; when celebration might be overwhelmed by satire; when sensibility swung between the extremes of enthusiasm and disgust; when the lover's quarrel between the writer and his people was most vigorously and creatively sustained.

The Irish Economy Since the War, 1946-51

PATRICK LYNCH

There were two distinct phases in the Irish economy in the six years between the end of the Second World War and 1951. In the first phase the government, with Mr de Valera as Taoiseach, sought to achieve rapid economic recovery from the trials and tribulations of war time; and the effort was remarkably successful. Neutrality during the war had been achieved and preserved; and a relatively high standard of living maintained, thanks to astute diplomatic skill by the government, to Mr Lemass as Minister for Supplies and to an easy access to Britain for the thousands of Irish workers who could not obtain jobs at home. It is a revealing insight into the bourgeois unconscious mind that emigration was sometimes described as a 'safety-valve', that is, a mechanism for avoiding radical reform or social revolution. Of course, the war left unsolved economic problems such as the standstill on wages and rising prices; and these grievances mounted to become vital issues in the first post-war general election in 1948 when the government was opposed by the traditional opposition parties Fine Gael, Labour and its dissident off-shoot National Labour, and also by a new party, Clann na Poblachta.

It was inevitable that a party such as Fine Gael, in parliamentary opposition for sixteen years, and parties, old and new,

H

that had never been in government before, should present the electorate with radical programmes or programmes that appeared, at least, to be wholeheartedly critical of the government. It was equally natural that the Fianna Fáil Party, however doctrinaire its original policies may have been years earlier, should, after sixteen years in government, be concerned mainly to defend in a practical way its performance, particularly its performance during the war. In the event, if dissatisfaction about the cost of living appeared to be the cause of the defeat of the Fianna Fáil government in 1948, the fate of its successor, the Inter-Party government, in 1951, was also to be associated with problems of rising prices resulting from inflation. No doubt, Mr de Valera might have made the distinction, with which I would agree, that in 1951 the Inter-Party government was to be the victim of its own inflation, whereas the inflation between 1946 and 1948 had been imported at a time when the Fianna Fáil government had little choice in the matter.

The second phase of the post-war economy began when the Inter-Party government came to office in 1948. As this government was composed of a variety of parties with, indeed, at first a certain variety of policies, some time had to elapse before a common economic approach could be framed, although an agreed programme was in fact published on the formation of the government. Not immediately could an ecumenical dialogue on economics be possible between, say, Mr James Dillon, whose views on tariff protection for industry had never been concealed, and Mr William Norton, leader of the Labour Party, whose views were known to be far from those of the Manchester school. It should be said, however, and emphatically, that such a consensus between Mr Dillon and Mr Norton was eventually reached. They disagreed on principles, not on practice.

The first year or so of the Inter-Party government showed that some ministers had outstanding skill as individual administrators, but a general and coherent policy was slow to appear. Mr Dillon, as Minister for Agriculture, immediately caught public attention because he had positive views on nearly all matters and could express them articulately with panache and colour. 'Flamboyant' said those who instinctively distrusted what was not dull. Much less rhetorical, but no less striking, was the late Mr Tim Murphy of the Labour Party, Minister for Local Government, who impressed by his sincerity and ability to get houses built, without claiming party political credit for his achievements.

The question remains, however: what eventually distinguished the Inter-Party government themselves from Fianna Fáil? This was to be a belief that capital investment by the state, based on the theories of John Maynard Keynes, could best solve the basic Irish economic problem of providing jobs for the thousands who were unemployed or who emigrated. State investment was to become the conspicuous feature of Inter-Party economic policies. The apotheosis came in the general election of 1951 when Inter-Party supporters could be heard at cross-roads political meetings holding forth on aspects of Cambridge employment theory, extolling the Land Project and public investment in general. This new economic faith composed differences of doctrine between right and left, between advocates of state intervention and devotees of private enterprise. Keynes had come to Kinnegad.

It must have been particularly hard for Mr Frank Aiken to find the Inter-Party ministers taking over Keynesian economics or 'inverted Keynesianism' as Professor George Duncan of Trinity College called it. It was commonly believed that, as Mr Aiken had in earlier years been a student of Major Douglas's social credit theories, he might have been regarded as, prematurely, a Keynesian theorist. Mr McGilligan's Budget of 1950, however, was the first explicit expression of Keynes in an Irish budget, and as Minister for Finance he became a formidable exponent of the relevance of employment theory to economic policy. He had no illusions about the cost of borrowing to the taxpayer. It would, he said, be £6 million in the next financial year. The Inter-Party Taoiseach, Mr. John A. Costello, left to others the relatively easy work of popularizing the new economics; he retained for himself the immensely difficult task of establishing its intellectual integrity and technical correctness.

The Fianna Fáil answer to the Inter-Party commitment to capital investment in 1950 and 1951 as a solution of Irish economic ills was a plausible one. Mr Lemass and Mr Aiken did not suggest that Keynesian theory was wrong; they took the view that it did not apply to Ireland at that particular time when, it seemed to them, the community was living beyond its income and consuming more than it was currently producing.

The general picture then of the Irish economy between 1946 and 1951 is one of remarkably rapid growth; but it was unbalanced growth in a context of inflation. In the 1950s correction of these inflationary tendencies was to cause stagnation. Neither the Fianna Fáil government from 1946 to 1948 nor the first Inter-Party government during the next three years was completely successful in reaching its objectives of national economic management. Indiscriminate protection for industry under Fianna Fáil had become a deterrent to industrial efficiency. Many of the Inter-Party government would have wished to recast these protective policies; but this proved impossible in the circumstances of the time without causing more unemployment. To industrial protection the Inter-Party government added a policy of public capital investment which began with the very best of intentions, but later became too undiscriminating between priorities; perhaps because of Marshall Aid, capital seemed deceptively cheap and too easily available.

The level of economic management during the war had been extremely high and solutions to difficult problems had been found with skill and resourcefulness. It was inevitable, however, that the effects of the war on Irish industry should be serious. Industrial output dropped because of shortages of raw materials; the quality of manufacturing plant was impaired, and there was the difficulty of securing parts for replacement. Employment did not fall to quite the same extent as output, but productivity diminished. The government so administered its policy of price control as to enable firms to retain their workers in spite of falling output. Industrial production showed its resilience soon after the end of the war and by 1946 the volume of production for all industry was nearly 7 per cent greater than it had been in 1936. It was 10 per cent greater in the case of the transportable goods industries.

Between 1946 and 1951, over 50,000 new jobs were created in Irish industry. Particular progress had been made in building and construction; thus, the industrial labour force had more than doubled since the policy for rapid industrialization had begun in 1932. This number, however, was less than half the total number employed in agriculture. It represented about 20 per cent of the total working population which, of course, was very low by contemporary European standards. Officially, in those immediate post-war years the prevailing political opinions of all parties favoured protection as a means of building up industry. It was argued that because of its large holding of external assets, Ireland, on a population basis, was one of the wealthiest countries in the world and, at the same time, a chronic loser of population through emigration. All industrially backward countries, it was said, favoured protection by tariffs and quotas. Moreover, it could be shown that there were fewer controls, perhaps, in Ireland than in many other European countries in the form of quota and currency restrictions. Nevertheless, there were voices in those early post-war years which suggested that tariffs and quotas and reliance on a small home market were hardly the best way to build competitive industries; that a form of protection, which made no provision for a scaling down of tariffs, was necessarily a barrier to increased industrial efficiency.

These voices, mainly those of the economists who had signed the Majority Report of the Banking Commission in 1938, received little attention between 1946 and 1951 from members of any political party save, perhaps, from Mr James Dillon who had always been a sort of economic Cassandra in Irish politics. The opinions of these economists in the later

1940s seemed echoes from the days of the Fiscal Enquiry Committee, and far removed from what governments wanted to hear between 1946 and 1951. They seemed much more like the economic orthodoxy prevailing in Ireland today among political leaders, civil servants and some economists. In the late 1940s, however, the liberalization of trade was being taken up by the O.E.E.C. following the granting of Marshall Aid, but to most people in Ireland in those post-war years it seemed unlikely that the tariff structure would ever be dismantled totally. Free trade then, even to Mr Dillon, must have appeared an unlikely Utopia.

One of the decisive steps taken by the first Inter-Party government in the promotion of industry was the creation of the Industrial Development Authority. The original members were non-civil servants with wide experience of financial, industrial and public life. Its fundamental responsibility was to plan, encourage and assist industrial development, though, and this is significant, it was also to examine the protectionist structure, a task for which the Department of Industry and Commerce seemed naturally unsuitable. Original critics of the Industrial Development Authority, of whom Mr Seán Lemass was one, were fair-minded enough to give the authority an opportunity of proving itself. This is, in fact, what the authority did. It has become one of the outstandingly successful instruments of economic policy, and it is doubtful if those who created it could have foreseen what it has achieved in helping to equip Ireland with an efficient and diversified industrial economy.

One of the less successful decisions of the new government in 1948 was to invite Sir John Milne, an expert British railway man, to examine the Irish transport problem. Not unnaturally, he saw the railway system as the essential core of Irish transport, even though the public was already clearly showing its preference for the flexibility of road transport. It was to be some years before Dr Beddy's Committee on Internal Transport exposed the fallacies of Sir John Milne's analysis.

In 1950 the Inter-Party government set up the Dollar

Exports Advisory Committee to examine methods of reducing the serious dollar deficit. As a result of its recommendations Córas Tráchtála was established to promote trade with the dollar area; its work has proved so successful that its activities have since been extended to all parts of the world.

Recovery of Irish agriculture from war conditions was necessarily slow, largely because of the lack of price incentive on the export markets, but by 1950 there were hopes that the traditional items of Irish agricultural produce were once again on the way towards securing an important place in the British market. Certainly, there was no lack of government schemes for helping the farmer. The main feature of the 1948 trade agreement negotiated by the Inter-Party government with Britain was a more direct linking of the prices paid for Irish beef with those of British beef. The Minister for Agriculture, Mr Dillon, set great store by that agreement, and so well he might, if his vision and that of Sir Stafford Cripps, the British Chancellor of the Exchequer, had been realized. Both saw the advantages of an integration of Irish and British agricultural economies. But pressure from British farm interests prevented its realization.

One of the more dramatic agricultural undertakings of the post-war period was the introduction in 1949 of the Land Rehabilitation Project. This was a large-scale effort to bring back into full production land which had remained idle through lack of capital and technical resources. The programme was expected to take about ten years to be completed and the real expenditure by the state was estimated to be in the region of £40 million, to be met, in part, from the proceeds in Irish currency of the dollar borrowings from the United States under the European Recovery Programme. There were at least two Irish views on Marshall Aid. One, the Department of Finance view, maintained that to avoid inflationary pressures the proceeds in Irish currency should not be used at all. In the event they were used. The Land Project which was financed in this way, aroused a good deal of enthusiasm among farmers as well as criticism from those

who argued that the returns from the investment might have
been more immediate if the project had been more selectively
directed—if the investment had concerned itself less with
marginal land, and more with improving the quality of the
better type of land. Here, of course, were legitimate political
judgements. Should the investment be used to improve the
social condition of small farmers or to promote the interests of
those who were already economically viable? As introduced,
the Land Project sought to assist the backward as well as the
economically advanced farmer. Even today, however, there
is lacking the evidence necessary for a final judgement of the
scheme as a whole.

Between 1939 and the end of the war there was hardly any
house building in Ireland; as a result there were very heavy
arrears and an intense demand for houses after 1945. The
immediate needs were estimated at about 110,000 new
dwellings, of which 70,000 represented houses to be provided
by local authorities. By 1950 the number of new houses completed had reached the figure of 12,000 a year which was
higher than any pre-war achievement, and there were high
hopes that this level of output would remove arrears of housing
in rural areas within a few years. The Dublin problem was, of
course, more difficult and was expected to take as long as ten
years to solve. This, of course, proved to be an under-estimate.

It was generally recognized after 1945 that the state would
continue to play an increasing economic part in the affairs of
the community. On the whole, however, the state's role was
haphazard and unsystematic, although by 1951 state-financed
capital schemes accounted for almost half of total domestic
capital formation. Nevertheless, the two principal parties,
Fianna Fáil and Fine Gael, were insistent that private enterprise was the motivating element in the Irish economy. As
Minister for Finance, Mr MacEntee said in 1952 . . . 'In a
free enterprise economy the Government cannot play a
dominant part in shaping the trend of economic and financial
affairs.' His predecessor, Mr McGilligan, had repeatedly expressed his detestation of state encroachment on the preserves

of the private individual. Yet, it was he who many years earlier had undertaken the Shannon Scheme as one of the first and the most successful of the more ambitious experiments in public enterprise in Great Britain or Ireland. Then, again, the new budgetary policy which he inaugurated in 1950 had the inevitable effect of facilitating more rational decisions in national economic development. This failure to reconcile systematically the precise role of public and private enterprise was to remain a feature of the economic policies of both Fianna Fáil and Fine Gael. The mixed economy of which both parties approved in practice, and to which both contributed, remained undefined. As a result, conflicts occurred between private and public enterprise which continued to inhibit the performance of both.

The manner in which post-war recovery was achieved had created some problems by 1951. Another balance of payments crisis had developed and the methods chosen to correct it were to have protracted deflationary consequences. If, therefore, quite a respectable growth rate was attained immediately after the war it tended to slow down after 1950. The rapid post-war rate of growth in the volume of industrial production had been due mainly to the low level from which development had begun and to the opportunities afforded for expansion in a protected home market. By 1951, the limits of profitable expansion were being reached for industries depending exclusively on the home market unless the standard of living of the rural community could be raised. The possibility of extending the market by seeking foreign markets was only beginning to be explored.

Between 1946 and 1953 industrial production increased by nearly 60 per cent and its employment content by almost 30 per cent. Over the same period, industrial growth in Britain was 43 per cent and the increase in the numbers employed only 15 per cent. It was, therefore, evident that if Irish industry were to equip itself to compete in export markets productivity would have to be greatly increased. Already by 1951 it had become almost a platitude to say that any very considerable reduction of the rate of emigration must depend on the growth of industry, but there were observers, especially in the O.E.E.C., who recited some of the obstacles whose removal would present difficulties. It was, indeed, not until seven years later in 1958, with the appearance of Mr Whitaker's *Economic Development* that these obstacles began to be clearly identified.

For over a quarter of a century industrial development had been helping to reduce emigration, but this social achievement of industry had to be set in a wider economic context. The total number of persons at work in the Republic in 1951 was only 12,000 more than in 1926, that is, 1 per cent more. There had been a net increase in non-agricultural employment of 159,000 and a decline of 147,000 in agricultural employment. The scope for employment on the land had been falling as it had been in every other country in western Europe. Employment in other occupations was increasing. The total number of persons employed in Ireland was remaining almost stationary; and all the time emigration was continuing at a rate of about 24,000 persons a year. The rate of industrial development was altogether insufficient to absorb the overflow from agriculture as well as the natural increase in population. In the period of unprecedented industrial progress from 1946 to 1951 the Irish economy created new jobs for only 800 persons a year. In other words, it offered jobs to one out of every thirty persons available for employment. This was some measure of the formidable task facing the government. Improvements, of course, were secured and advances made, but no completely satisfactory solution was found to the basic problem.

Little wonder, that in these years, a scepticism was growing as to whether these problems were soluble at all. Pessimists were talking of the death-wish of an Irish economy which to survive had to be subsidized by high emigration and by the use of the savings of a former generation. Others urged that the reciprocal relationship of the Irish and British economies should be faced, that it would be to the advantage of both if each recognized explicitly its dependence on the other. But the idea of an Anglo-Irish Free Trade Area was premature then, and no one had yet contemplated the possibility of Ireland and Britain participating in a wider economic union in Europe.

Apart from efforts to increase the scope of public capital investment, the policies of the late 1940s remained much the same as before. It would be quite wrong, of course, to use hind-sight in criticism of individual policies; but especially after 1948 there was a long delay in effectively creating a satisfactory organization for the promotion of tourism, even though that industry could be shown to be third in importance in the list of sources of external income. There seems to have been a belief that a competitive tourist industry could have established itself spontaneously.

In 1945 the immediate economic objectives of the government under Mr de Valera had been to restore the economy from the effects of the war and to avoid inflation. In general, the first objective was attained more easily and more quickly than many had expected. As already stated, by 1946 a great deal had been done to increase output and employment. The second objective, however, was to prove more elusive. Indeed, it was in 1946 that inflationary forces began to become even more difficult to repel than they had been during the war. The government was clearly alarmed at the increases in prices, and the continuing shortage of such essential raw material as coal produced widespread discontent. In 1946 and 1947 it must have been apparent to the government that there was plenty of dissatisfaction with its economic policies; and all this must have seemed very thankless after what had been achieved in more difficult circumstances during the war in the management of the economy. In the belief that the prevailing inflation would be temporary, as had been the inflation after the First World War, the Minister for Finance introduced food subsidies to keep down the cost of essential supplies. This belief that the inflation would be temporary was proved wrong; there was a continuing need for the subsidies which imposed an increasing burden on current taxation. Rarely had any piece of budgetary machinery played a bigger part in politics. The supplementary budget of 1947—another counter-inflationary measure—was to become a weapon with which to berate the government as the main issue in the general election of 1948. When the Inter-Party government assumed office in February 1948 it was inevitable that they should promise the repeal of the supplementary budget introduced by Fianna Fáil; in due course reductions in taxation did, in fact, take place. Whether such reductions were justifiable economically in an inflationary situation remained a problem for the academic economists.

The war had had a striking effect on Ireland's holdings of sterling assets. Between the First and Second World Wars Ireland's foreign payments were slightly in excess of foreign earnings, and there had been a modest, indeed insignificant, drawing on sterling assets. Between 1939 and 1946 Ireland's foreign earnings exceeded payments by £162 million. The gross total of Irish sterling assets in 1946 was probably around £430 million. From 1947 to 1952 there were deficits in the balance of payments amounting to about £160 million, which were met from loans and grants under the European Recovery Programme, from capital imports and from the liquidation of about £35 million of sterling assets. On this reckoning the level of Irish sterling assets in the early 1950s was around £400 million. The net creditor position, when account was taken of Ireland's liabilities under the European Recovery Programme, sterling debt and external capital invested in Ireland, was about £120 million.

There was nothing doctrinaire about the post-war economic policies of the Fianna Fáil government. Perhaps the necessity of countering the immediate threat of inflation left little scope at that stage for the development of detailed policy statements. The arguments of the Majority Report of the Banking Commission had left their mark. The bad winter of 1947 brought shortages of coal and wheat; there was even a threat of maize in the flour. The complaints of profiteering continued.

In the establishment of the Central Bank and in the debates

on that measure the Fianna Fáil ministers had shown that the Secretary of the Department of Finance, Mr McElligott, had apparently been entirely successful in confirming in, or converting to, economic orthodoxy, any sceptics who remained in the Fianna Fáil leadership. In economics, however, Fianna Fáil had never really been a radical party. The doctrines it had brought to office in 1932 had been largely derived from Arthur Griffith and the nineteenth-century German economist, List. Probably the most radical economic thinker in the party had been the late Joseph Connolly, but by 1945 he had long since retired from politics to public administration, though he often told me that he remained convinced that the level of economic management of the community by the government was still too low.

In the 1948 general election Mr MacBride's party, Clann na Poblachta, came forward with an ambitious programme, especially on the economic side, rather resembling that of Fianna Fáil in 1932. Many of Mr MacBride's supporters held, with deep conviction, that the link with sterling was the root cause of all Irish economic troubles though they remained silent and obscure in showing why. Mr MacBride himself, however, was more moderate than his fellow reformers on this subject. In due course, when he became a member of the first Inter-Party government, he was to become, almost alone, an ardent advocate of economic planning. The Fine Gael Party placed most stress on agriculture, and the Labour Party was concerned mainly with the effect of increased prices and the cost of living, and expressed their concern about alleged excessive profit making by industrialists. The defeat of the Fianna Fáil government in 1948 was generally regarded by commentators as an expression of discontent with its economic policies, especially in cities and towns. The defeat was probably welcomed by ministers who were weary after so many difficult years in office. Certainly, many of them were glad of an opportunity of independent reflection on the implications of new situations in the party's economic and social policies. Mr Lemass, in particular, never concealed his enjoyment in being able from the opposition front bench to turn his vast experience to use in criticizing the policies of the new government.

A White Paper on Ireland's long-term programme in connection with the European Recovery Programme was published in January 1949 by the Inter-Party government. There was nothing strikingly original in it. Its span was for the subsequent four years and in general outline it contemplated Ireland continuing to be a producer of food mainly for the British market. It made limited and cautious proposals for industrial development and placed rather excessive emphasis on afforestation and electricity development—two lines upon which Mr MacBride's party placed great store. Up to this time the main stress of Inter-Party policies in economic matters had been on agriculture and afforestation. Indeed, the Land Project was seen as a new force in rural development, and was presented ably by the Minister for Agriculture, Mr Dillon. Removing the rocks from Connemara may have been bad economics for Irish adherents of the Manchester school, but to many people emotionally involved in the west of Ireland and its people it was the best news since the activities of the Congested Districts Board.

In September 1949 the British government took the momentous decision to devalue the pound sterling, and Ireland had little option but to follow suit, describing the step as 'the course of least disadvantage'. The act of devaluation seemed to justify some of the more extreme aspects of the original policy of Clann na Poblachta. From then onwards the case for what was called 'repatriation of sterling assets' was made unceasingly both by those who understood what the process involved and by very many who assumed that repatriation could be achieved in the Central Bank by the stroke of a Governor's pen.

In the summer of 1950 the Korean war began and for the remainder of that year it was becoming evident that inflationary pressures were driving up prices. The government found itself facing the same kind of criticism as the Fianna Fáil government had been meeting in 1947 and early 1948.

In January 1951 the Prices Advisory Body was established, but the inflation continued. The Inter-Party government was defeated in the 1951 general election and Fianna Fáil returned to office. There were, of course, more than economic issues in that election, but for the rest of the year a great debate ensued on economic policies and techniques, largely on the issue of capital investment which had appeared to divide the Inter-Party government from Fianna Fáil during the previous three years. The year ended with the appearance of the Central Bank Report still strongly arguing that excessive capital investment had produced the inflation which was the root cause of the country's troubles. Cost inflation, domestically stimulated, was said to be the villain. Keynes, fully employed in Merrion Street, had not yet reached the bankers in Foster Place.

The next seven years were to be singularly lean ones for Ireland, first under the Fianna Fáil government of 1951 and later the second Inter-Party government. These were to be years of stagnation in which the unceasing struggle against inflation displaced economic growth as an attainable object of policy. It might be said and, indeed, often was said, especially by Mr Seán MacEntee, that financial order, particularly in the balance of payments, had to be restored before progress could be resumed. In the event, the resumption of progress was postponed till 1958. The Capital Investment Advisory Committee and Mr Whitaker in *Economic Development* were then pointing towards a more constructive and effective management of the economy. Most of the old policies of previous governments were shown by Whitaker to have failed. A responsible and productive programme of public capital investment would now justify repatriation of sterling assets provided due regard was had to its effect on the balance of payments. Industry would be encouraged by incentives to seek markets abroad. The machinery of government should be adapted to facilitate development planning for economic growth. But in 1951 barren years lay ahead, culminating in the payments crisis of 1956, before such proposals were incorporated in the First Programme for Economic Expansion in 1958.

The years immediately before 1958 were not entirely arid. The tax reliefs on exports introduced in the 1956 Finance Act were indeed to have a most fruitful effect on the pattern of future economic growth.

SOURCES

Annual Reports of Central Bank of Ireland.
B. O'Kennedy, 'Apropos of Dr Duignan', *The Bell*, X/5, August 1945.
'Economic Survey of the Republic of Ireland', *The Statist*, 3 Feb. 1951.
P. Lynch, 'The Economist and Public Policy', *Studies*, Autumn 1953.
'The Economy of Ireland', *The Statist*, 24 Oct. 1953.
'The Finance Attitude', *Administration*, Autumn 1954.
    T. K. Whitaker, 'Capital Formation, Saving and Economic Progress', *Journal of the Statistical and Social Inquiry Society of Ireland*, 1956.
    First, Second and Third Reports of the Capital Investment Advisory Committees, Stationery Office, Dublin 1951–8.

Conclusion

T. DESMOND WILLIAMS

The world of 1939 differed immensely from the world of 1969—indeed often from that of 1951. For most countries in Europe, at least, the war and its outcome provided the great division. And this extended to national as much as to international politics. The stimulus of war altered the balance of power and influence just as much within national society as between the different states themselves—and this alteration was radical. Affluence arrived with war—at least for the masses and for many women. Economic and social structures underwent substantial changes in nearly all the countries directly involved in the far-reaching conflict of the Second World War. In many states, political and social upheavals of a revolutionary character took place—in France, in Germany and elsewhere in Europe; in England, social levelling on a wide scale was gradually accomplished though many of the old landmarks were retained. War can be a mighty engine for change. Of course the belligerents involved are more affected by its impetus than neutrals on the periphery. Thus Switzerland, Sweden, Portugal and Spain, despite their diverse social and political arrangements, emerged in 1945 more recognizably what they had been six years earlier than did Britain for instance, or France.

What of Ireland?—also a neutral state, but even more

remote from the stress of war. And what happened to her after that war, what of any serious consequence in the following six years?

Now, if there is any certainty for historians, it is the fact of change. *Eppure si muove*—all the time. But such change can, over a considerable period, be almost imperceptible. Sometimes, too, the longer drawn out and more persistently hidden the rumbling, the more sudden and striking the stir and din when the ferment erupts. Any observer of those years may, as far as Ireland is concerned, find it difficult to detect indications of the social, intellectual and moral revolution that is now upon us—or even of the political changes that knock more timidly on the door of the present generation.

Looking at the entire period from 1939 to 1951, certain specific fields may be plotted for consideration of significant change :

(1) Ireland's position in the world at large;

(2) Domestic politics;

(3) Social atmosphere and practice;

(4) Church and state;

(5) Developments in education and intellectual life generally;

(6) Progress, or otherwise, towards the unification of North and South;

(7) Finally the respective claims of youth, middle and old age to influence the formation of policy in all aspects of life.

If one starts at the end of the period, in 1951, it is probably true to say that Ireland meant less in the world of journalism and reportage than it did in earlier ages. Ireland had been news everywhere during the nineteenth century; and this continued for many years of the twentieth. There were at least two reasons for this : Ireland, as part of the British empire, with Dublin as that empire's second city, figured in much imperial history, even when, or more particularly because, the country was in revolt. There was also the fact that continued emigration from Ireland to the United States made the Irish significant there too. In diplomacy the Irish question was crucial on both sides of the Atlantic. And this went on until at least 1922. But even after that the role of Ireland in the development of dominion and Commonwealth lent her an international significance—particularly in the evolution of such dominions as Canada, Australia, New Zealand, South Africa and India. Ireland, in fact, had a key vote in this circle. Irish political controversy also was relevant to the developing history of those dominions—and this was still so throughout the war up to the declaration of the Republic and its secession from the Commonwealth. Even at the League of Nations Ireland could play a greater role than she can in its successor organization. In such an institution, where member states are so much more numerous, Tanzania and Cyprus would appear to exercise far more influence than Ireland ever could. The League of Nations was essentially a European structure—in contrast to the Afro-Asian character which the United Nations has now largely assumed. The role of the Irish in United States politics could not be said, by 1951, to have disappeared. After all, Kennedy was elected in 1960. Yet Kennedy's election signified the coming of age of the Irish Americans. They played some role as a separate element in American politics up till and during the Second World War. But even then they were moving towards representing a more specifically American than Irish attitude. And from 1924, and the restrictive emigration act of that year, the proportionate influence and inflow of people from Ireland has gradually been reduced.

The interest of the English in Ireland or in Irish questions dwindled rapidly after the Treaty. De Valera, by virtue of the role he played from 1916 down to 1948, remained a personality of international repute. The successful maintenance of the objectives of neutrality between 1939 and 1945 put the seal on independence. A great historian once stressed the dictum that 'all policy is foreign policy'. Extreme as this thesis may seem, the putting to the test of Ireland's right to pursue her own foreign policy in the context of fierce and unremitting hostilities all around her established her full sovereignty and also allowed for the prosecution of an isolationalist policy. This was completed by Mr Costello's decision to leave the Commonwealth as well as to declare a Republic. Two things were established during the war: Ireland's right as a nation to pursue her own national interests and the power to pursue them. But by 1951, it looked as if Irish influence in international affairs had declined. There was also very little evidence at the time that Irish governments were interested in what had been happening abroad. Of course Ireland, as a neutral, was not immediately invited to the fifty-nation San Francisco conference of 1945 which laid down the constitution of the United Nations. Subsequent admission depended upon agreement in the Security Council. Ireland was proposed after 1946 but was excluded by the Soviet veto along with ten other states. It was not until 1955 that she was admitted as a result of a package deal between the U.S.S.R. and the Western Powers. In any event, neutrals had little influence or popularity with states that had been involved in the war. It is difficult to see that Ireland lost anything significant by her temporary exclusion. She arrived, anyhow, in time for the Suez controversy and for the initial advance of the Afro-Asian group in the latter part of the 'fifties.

Ireland also continued an apparently neutralist policy with her decision in April 1949 to remain out of the North Atlantic Treaty Organization. The reason given looked somewhat spurious: namely, the alleged guarantee which that treaty would give to the maintenance of the territorial integrity of Northern Ireland as part of the North Atlantic Treaty area. This was the specific contribution made by Seán MacBride—

his intervention here being of far more importance than the role he played or did not play in determining the formal establishment of the Republic and secession from the Commonwealth. One consequence of the refusal to adhere to N.A.T.O. has been argued. It concerned the European problem as it subsequently developed. If we had been in N.A.T.O. we would have had more constant contact of an effective kind with the European states: with France, with Germany, Italy and Belgium. Our diplomatic connection with European states might have been stronger; and this might have had some relevance for future possibilities within the context of the European economic community. As it was, political connection with Europe had to be established at the tail of Britain and within the sole context of the 1965 free trade agreement concluded with her. Of course, public opinion might not have accepted adherence to N.A.T.O., the tradition of neutrality having firmly established itself during the war. In fact, N.A.T.O., as we now know, would not have brought us into any war, and it is not even clear that it would necessarily have involved an abandonment of neutrality if it had ever had to be tested.

It must be added that Ireland after the war was involved in the economic recovery of Europe through O.E.E.C. and Irish civil servants like Ambassador Boland co-operated closely with Hammarskjold (also representing a neutral state) in the work of that organization. Perhaps indeed the partnership of Boland and Hammarskjold was not without its influence upon the subsequent selection of Boland as President of the General Assembly of the United Nations, about ten years later.

There was no great change in government from 1939 to 1948. De Valera and Fianna Fáil still continued to run the country and de Valera's patience, skill and success in executing neutrality probably prolonged the 'age of de Valera' (as indeed the whole period from 1932 to 1948 can be fairly described). 1948 was significant in that it involved a change of government and provided the country and Fianna Fáil itself with a desirable escape from sixteen years of one party rule. This

benefited probably all the parties concerned and it was good
for the state in general. Too many years of domination are
bad for a democracy and also for those in power. The inter-
ruption of Fianna Fáil's supremacy allowed for the airing of
fresh views and fresher personalities. Whatever the defects of
coalition government (and there were several), it made parliamentary government revive. There was a strong opposition
and a new administration. This was good for the civil service.
New ideas, particularly concerning economic development,
penetrated the bureaucracy and public life generally. In
some respects, indeed, there were anticipations of the kind of
planning ideas which were to be formulated in the new economic programmes of 1957 and 1961. There were advantages,
too, for Fianna Fáil, which could be charged with lethargy
and arrogance in the early post-war years. This was almost
inevitable, but it must be remembered too that Ireland did not
disentangle herself from the economic consequences of war
until at least 1948. Fianna Fáil could then take a new look at
itself. Most important of all, the policies of the new Costello
government enabled Seán Lemass and his party to initiate
their retreat from the policy of protectionism, which had
proved valid through the accident of war, but which, even
before 1939, had begun in part to appear out of date. As
regards the ultimate development of the industrial economy,
the rise in the standard of living and the arrival of a more
affluent society (for those who remained in the country), the
new policies and the new personalities in ministerial posts all
provided a broader outlook for subsequent governments including those of Fianna Fáil in 1951 and 1957. There were
certainly novel openings and novel departures, though the
changes were to appear more obvious later than at the time
itself. So the period 1948 to 1951 may be regarded as the end
of a political era and the beginning of an economic one. There
was indeed some talk around 1951 that de Valera would
shortly resign—from political life—primarily for reasons of
health. This did not happen, but the new tendencies, some of
which were in obvious contrast with the philosophy of the

older world (for which he stood), circulated more rapidly and finally surfaced with the arrival of Lemass as Taoiseach, in 1959.

The years 1948 to 1951 were accompanied by the opening of a continuous debate on the virtues and defects of coalition government. The evils of coalition were constantly stressed by de Valera. He argued that one could never have strong and courageous government under the conditions of a coalition. The weaker party in the government would always be in a position to hold the strongest group up to ransom. Unpopular measures, however necessary, he asserted, could not be introduced in these circumstances. Coalition also tended to dissolve the principle of collective responsibility in the cabinet. There was, indeed, some evidence of this development in 1950 and 1951—when the contrasting electoral interests of Fine Gael, Labour and Clann na Poblachta reflected themselves in the contradictory speeches of the leaders. Here, too, another theoretical problem of government was introduced—though only sporadically in these years. It began to look impossible at that stage that any party would be able to secure an overall majority in the Dáil and thus form an effective government. The advantages and disadvantages of proportional representation were raised. No firm decisions were taken or attitudes adopted but the contours of subsequent controversy on this matter were appearing on the horizon.

The period 1938 to 1951 witnessed a decline in the potential influence of those forces opposed to constitutional government. The I.R.A. survived the war in a limited sense; but as an organization capable of securing mass support among the young, it was virtually finished by the end of this period. There was still to be another I.R.A., which erupted between 1951 and 1961. It is, of course, impossible to predict anything with absolute certainty in history. All the same, as from the end of the war, there was little place for this illegal organization as an instrument of either domestic or external influence (in respect of partition) as long as it refused to accept the rules of the constitutional game. It had sentenced itself or had been sentenced to the role of a small and ineffective minority protest group.

Still, from the historical viewpoint, the role of the I.R.A., its relation to government, its place in the conduct of neutrality, and the personal tragedy involved may perhaps command more attention than has so far been accorded it. It was out-witted and outmanoeuvred at every point by de Valera and by his Minister for Justice, Gerry Boland. The methods employed were various; the velvet glove until early in 1940 and more of an iron fist from then onwards. Those circles inspired by hostility to any connection with Britain were fundament-ally appeased by the policy of neutrality to which the British under Churchill had so strongly objected. There must have been some conflict of conscience within Fianna Fáil about these matters. Members of that party had been in internment camps less than twenty years back. They now instituted similar institutions. Military tribunals too were re-established; men died on hunger strike not only during but after the war; and others were shot, after sentence by the tribunals. There must, too, have been a sad and seemingly fruitless loss of life and waste of opportunity. But this is the destiny of many revolu-tionary causes and the men who outlast them, or the youth which inherits belatedly the ideals of yesteryear. Anyhow, Russell, Ryan, McCaughy, Plant, McNeil, Kerins and Darcy will merit some consideration from future historians interested in the changes that came about in Ireland during this period.

As regards partition, only a few words need be said in respect of any significant developments between the beginning of the war and 1951. The war itself made no difference; each government (in the North as well as the South) took care to avoid entering into troubled waters from 1939 until the end of hostilities. Each solved its I.R.A. problems in its own way; each too had its internment camps; there was more activity in the South than in the North, but the result was the same. Each government took up its traditional stand concerning its claims, as dating back to 1920 and 1921. There were no pogroms in Belfast as had been the case in 1922 or 1935. External policy was not affected and the status quo was maintained up to 1949. Then there was a resuscitation of activity in the South. Following upon the declaration of the Republic, Mr Costello's government promoted a campaign designed to attract world attention to the seeming injustice of the division of Ireland. This was partly in response to the decision of Mr Attlee's Labour administration to introduce by act of parliament a guarantee that no change should be made regarding the constitutional connection between Northern Ireland and Britain without the consent of the former. A somewhat grandiloquent statement was made by the Taoiseach that 'we would hit Britain in her pride, purse and pound'. Mr Costello undoubtedly intended such an effect; but he cannot have believed in its efficacy for very long. The anti-partition committee was active for a number of years, without results. Here there was much a-doing about nothing. Government and opposition both participated in this campaign. Meetings and pronunciamentos were organized in Dublin, London and, indeed, on wider fields. The statisticians, polemicists and politicians all made their contribution. A pamphlet was produced with the assistance of the Department of External Affairs. Geoffrey Bing, an English M.P. of left-wing disposition, Presbyterian in origin and born in Co. Down, collaborated in the production of the pamphlet. On one occasion, an unusual scene took place at the Council of Europe in which Irish delegates of different parties participated, de Valera included. This may have pleased the Irish back home but it certainly did nothing to impress other delegates concerned with what to them were bigger and more significant issues. Partition had become one of the great clichés of Irish politics; and to preach against it was as obvious as preaching against sin. No one ever really expected much to be achieved. De Valera himself, shortly after his departure from government in 1948, had undertaken a world-wide tour during which, among other things, he tried to bring the same message home to other countries, particularly those in which the largest Irish populations were to be found. Some British politicians, mainly among the Labour Party, were concerned but they were few and far between. The Irish no longer exercised any significant and settled influence in the British political system. Still a few individuals abstained from supporting the Republic of Ireland Act in 1949 : and these included Harold Wilson. Some Irish-Americans did take an interest but they proved embarrassing when they arrived to offer Mr Costello arms and money on condition that they would be used for the purpose of bringing pressure to bear against what was then described as the 'Six-County government'. These offers were, of course, not accepted; and it may be assumed that some of these funds eventually found their way into other hands, more prepared to try the argument of force.

How much change was there in social life—its atmosphere and practice? Well, many changes occurred in the balance of population between town and country, and in the pace of emigration. This has been discussed elsewhere in this series in a detailed way. Certainly the war had immense influence on the speed and direction of emigration. The Irish had always been used to the fact, at least for 150 years. The significant point between 1939 and 1951 was that Britain was almost the sole objective of the migrant during the war years; and this trend did not disappear. In fact it was to continue at a very high rate right on into the early 'sixties. Such a depletion of human resources obviously altered the conditions of rural life. The young left and the old stayed behind. Remittances assisted the survival of the homestead to some extent, and it is difficult to detect any real change in the conservative attitudes of the countryside up till 1951. New Irish 'ghettoes' were speedily being formed especially in Birmingham, Manchester and London. This development was haphazard and unorganized. The attitudes and morals of the British cities were not conveyed back to Ireland immediately; and it was only in subsequent years that radical changes began to be introduced or advocated in respect of the life of Irishmen in Ireland. The 'permissive' attitudes had to wait for the middle 'sixties and in 1951 motor-cars were rare enough in some parts of the west, south or midlands. Some tired British citizens, disgusted with the threat of socialist government, did invade rural Ireland towards the end of the 'forties. They were also in search of the red meat denied them from 1940 until 1950, but tourism on a mass scale had not appeared—though some ventures were initiated with a growing tourist trade in view. All in all, society in rural areas remained pretty much such as it had been before the war. The same kind of discussions took place in the pubs, the faces of the same politicians at parliamentary or county council level re-appeared at every election, and youth still took its humble and orthodox place until it left for foreign parts.

The relations of Church and state did not alter significantly. Much had been made of the importance of Dr Browne's 'mother and child' scheme and of the intervention of the bishops in this affair. But there was nothing new about the relationship. The conditions of coalition government, the tactics of the most successful trade union of all, the Irish Medical Association, Dr Browne's own misinterpretation of episcopal negotiation, the Minister's own peculiar relationship with the leader of his party, Seán MacBride, and the special phraseology of Archbishop McQuaid—all these gave this particular political crisis a character which it would have lacked under different circumstances and with different personalities involved. Churchmen were, in general, conservative, as they had been before the war. They and their flock seemed content with existing arrangements. There was little or no change of any importance in the educational system. T.C.D. and U.C.D. kept apart from each other but the acrimonious controversies of later years were only beginning to be expressed with the advent of Dr Michael Tierney as president of University College in 1947. Some lay Catholic voices were heard in the primary, secondary and vocational schools. But the altercations were minor and the notes muted. The reaction to the Browne scheme and its defeat were perhaps relevant in so far as fresh views were widely expressed. Social welfare policies were more implied than formally asserted.

For example there was the formula produced by de Valera and Cardinal D'Alton to cover Dr Ryan's version of the Browne scheme. Face was saved on both sides—for Church and state—but in practice, as far as mother-and-child were concerned, the essentials of the very limited Browne scheme were secured. There were, in fact, no great signs of any national pressure for change involving tension between Church and state.

This also applied to the world of intellectual life. On the whole the problems of censorship and sex, let alone the issue of the Irish language, were being analysed and resolved along the lines raised in intellectual debate before 1939. True, younger men were writing, but they had little more to say than their older contemporaries in earlier years. Some of them wrote very well, but the causes advocated or challenged remained pretty much the same.

Index

Aiken, Frank, Minister for the co-ordination of defence, 23–24, 42–43, 44, 45; and Keynesian economics, 187–88

Alexander, Field Marshall, Lord, 71, 73

Andrews, J. M., 55

Anglo-Irish Trade Agreement of 1938, 1, 3, 4, 13, 28, 30, 149, 152

Attlee, Clement, 64, 73, 143, 209

Bates, Sir Dawson, 62

Becket, Samuel, 167, 170, 173, 179, 180

Beddy, Dr James, 108, 123, 190

Belfast air raids, 57–59

Blowick, Joseph, 156

Boland, F. H., 137, 205.

Bowen, Elizabeth, 167, 173

Brennan, Robert, 25, 26

Brooke, Sir Basil, his activities in Stormont, 60–61

Browne, Dr Noel, as a member of Clann na Poblachta, 69; and the mother and child scheme, 76–78, 162, 163, 211, 212; his resignation as Minister, 79

Chamberlain, Neville, and conscription, 12; and defence, 16; and the restoration of the ports, 41

Churchill, Winston, 18, 20, 22, 23, 24, 33, 208

Clarke, Austin, 167, 169, 170–71, 174, 176, 177, 180

Colum, Padraic, 168, 169

Connolly, James, 96, 105, 154

Constitution of 1922, 8, 111–12, 113, 114, 147

Constitution of 1937, 1, 8, 13, 14, 41, 81, 111–14, 117, 119, 139, 147

Corkery, Daniel, 167, 168

Cosgrave, W. T., on Ireland's defence policy during the Second World War, 44, 47; and Church-state relations, 113; retires from Fine Gael leadership, 153; otherwise mentioned, 81, 115, 116

Costello, John A., on Irish neutrality during the Second World War, 7–8; and the External Relations Act, 65, 71–74, 140–41, 204; as Taoiseach, 118, 161, 187–88; and the mother and child scheme, 78; dissolves the Dáil, 79; his attitude to partition, 136, 209; otherwise mentioned, 206, 210

Craig, James, see Lord Craigavon

Craigavon, Lord, and conscription, 12, 53; wins his last general election, 52; prises benefits for the North from Britain, 52; and the

Local Defence Force, 54; his death, 55; and Church-state relations, 115
Cripps, Sir Stafford, 140, 191
Cronin, Anthony, 173
Currency Commission, 29–30

Derrig, Thomas, and the restoration of the Irish language 81, 83, 86, 91; and school examinations, 89
De Valera, Eamon, and the 1938 Anglo-Irish negotiations, 1–5, 41, 52, 152; and the Second World War, 6–8 12, 14, 15, 16, 17, 18, 19, 20, 21, 22, 23, 24, 25, 26, 39, 42, 44, 45, 47, 49, 117, 205; and party politics, 10, 148, 151, 157, 159, 164, 165, 207; and Hitler's death, 14, 67; and the External Relations Act, 70, 74; his attitude to the restoration of the Irish language, 81–82; establishes emergency government, 111; attitude of Church authorities towards him, 116; his foreign policy often at variance with Catholic attitudes, 116–17; his party defeated but later returned to office, 118; his views on membership of U.N.O., 134–35; and partition, 39, 136, 209; at the 1947 Conference on European Economic Co-operation, 137–38; and party organization, 149–50; and post-war government, 185, 186, 195; otherwise mentioned, 68, 89, 139, 151, 203, 206, 212

Devlin, Denis, 175–76
Dillon, James, and the Second World War, 8, 15, 44; on teaching through Irish, 85; questions the Taoiseach about the status of Ireland, 139; expelled by Fine Gael, 153; as Minister for Agriculture, 75, 165, 186–87, 191, 198; his views on tariff protection, 186; his attitude to the Irish economy, 189–90
Donnellan, Michael, 156
Duignan, Dr John, Bishop of Clonfert, 116, 118

Farren, Robert, 168, 169, 174, 177

Goertz, Captain Hermann, and the I.R.A., 17–18; his arrest, 22
Gray, David, as American minister in Dublin, 20; advises Roosevelt, 24
Greacen, Robert, 174
Green, F. L., 59

Hartnett, Noel, 79
Hempel, Eduard, and Hitler's death, 14; and the German Secret Service, 18, 19; and the I.R.A., 25
Henderson, Tommy, 58
Hitler, Adolf, 14, 15, 18, 45, 46, 47
Hutchinson, Pearse, 173
Hyde, Douglas, 1, 151
Ireland Act, 65, 75
I.R.A., 9, 10, 11, 12, 16, 17, 18, 22, 23, 25, 46, 50, 52, 59, 207, 208

Iremonger, Valentin, 173, 174, 177

Johnston, Denis, 176

Kavanagh, Patrick, 173, 174–75

Keynes, John Maynard, 187, 199

Kiely, Benedict, 173

Kinsella, Thomas, 173

Kyle, Senator Sam, his influence on trade union differences, 103

Larkin, James, (junior), expelled from the Labour Party, 101; open letter on the occasion of his father's death, 106

Larkin, Jim, as general secretary of the Workers' Union of Ireland, 96, 99; elected to the Dáil, 100–101; otherwise mentioned, 105, 106, 107

Lavin, Mary, 173, 178

Lemass, Seán, and the 1938 Anglo-Irish Trade Agreement, 4; as Minister for Supplies, 31, 185; introduces Industrial Relations Bill, 107; representing Ireland at 1947 Conference on European Economic Co-operation, 137; his views on Keynesian economics, 188; is a keen critic of the government, 197–98; otherwise mentioned, 82, 106, 190, 206, 207

Lynch, Jack, on education, 87

MacBride, Seán, and Clann na Poblachta, 69, 158–59; and the External Relations Act, 70–71, 72, 73; on N.A.T.O. and partition, 136–37, 204–205; featured in *Life*, 160; advocates 'representative government', 161; as Minister for External Affairs, 162; and the Irish economy, 197; otherwise mentioned, 198, 211

MacCartan, Patrick, 157

MacDermott, J. C., 57

MacEntee, Seán, and the 1938 Anglo-Irish Trade Agreement, 3; as Minister for Industry and Commerce, 31, 96, 99; opposed to social benefits scheme, 118; as Minister for Finance, 192, 199

MacEoin, General Seán, 8, 157

McGilligan, Patrick, and neutrality, 15; his questions on war-time policy, 44; his description of the wrong kind of neutrality, 47; as Minister for Finance, 76, 187, 192–93

Macken, Walter, 177

McLaverty, Michael, 178

MacLiammóir, Micheál, 168, 176

MacMahon, Bryan, 178

MacManus, Francis, 167, 178, 179

McSparran, James, leader of the Nationalist Party in the North, 65

McQuaid, Dr J. C., Archbishop of Dublin, 87, 211

Maffey, Sir John, and German espionage in Dublin, 18; as British representative in Dublin, 20–21, 25

Milne, Sir John, 190

Molloy, M. J., 177

Montague, John, 173
Moore, Brian, 59
Mulcahy, General Richard, not chosen as Taoiseach, 69; as Minister for Education, 92; his advocacy of an Anglo-Irish military alliance, 153; leader of Fine Gael, 154
Murphy, T. J., 101, 187

Norton, William, and neutrality, 8; and the External Relations Act, 72, 73; and Jim Larkin, 100, 101; sets up commission on emigration and population problems, 123; as leader of the Labour Party, 155, 163; his views on economics, 186; otherwise mentioned, 47, 106

O'Brien, Conor Cruise, 173
O'Brien, Flann, 179–80
O'Brien, Kate, 167, 178, 179
O'Brien, William, as general secretary of the Irish Transport and General Workers' Union, 96–106
O'Casey, Seán, 167, 176, 177
O'Connor, Frank, 169, 170, 173, 177
Ó Deirg, Thomas *see* Thomas Derrig
O'Donnell, Peadar, 173
O'Duffy, General Eoin, 22

O'Faolain, Seán, 167, 169, 170, 171–73, 177
O'Flaherty, Liam, 167, 169, 170, 173, 177
O'Kelly, Seán T., 157
O'Malley, Donagh, on education, 89
O'Sullivan, Professor John Marcus, and the restoration of the Irish language, 86

Partition, 1, 2, 6, 39, 49, 70, 74, 75, 109, 117, 136–37, 208–209, 210

Roosevelt, Franklin D., 16, 18, 20, 23, 24
Russell, Seán, 10, 18, 208
Ryan, Frank, 18, 23, 208

Shaw, G. B., 142
Stephens, James, 167, 180
Stuart, Francis, 178–79

Thompson, Lt. Col. Hall, 64

Wall, Mervyn, 179, 180–84
Warnock, J. E., 55
Wartime imports and exports, 34–37
Whitaker, T. K., 194, 199
Williamson, Bruce, 174

Yeats, W. B., 167, 168, 169, 174, 175, 177